MW00584348

# The
# Northeast Passage

A guide to the seas and wildlife islands of Arctic Siberia

## Tony Soper

Venture Books

Third edition, revised 2020
First published 2016

Text copyright © Tony Soper

The author and publisher have made every effort to ensure the accuracy of the information in this book at the time of going to press. They cannot accept any responsibility for any loss, injury, or inconvenience resulting from the use of information contained in this guide.

All rights reserved. No part of this publication may be reproduced, stored in a retrieval system, or transmitted in any form or by any means, electronic, mechanical, photocopying, recording or otherwise without the prior consent of the publisher.

British Library Cataloguing in Publication Data
A catalogue record for this book is available from the British Library
ISBN-13: 978-0-9553801-5-0

Maps: Terence Crump

Project managers: Diane Reynolds and Jane Galer

venturebooks@icloud.com

Cover image credits:
  *Front cover* Martin Enckell
  *Back cover* Martin Enckell (Polar bear), Tony Soper (IB *Yamal* in the Franz Josef archipelago)

# Contents

With a lot of care, close pack ice is navigable by a well-found vessel.
Multi-year ice with pressure ridges is a job for an icebreaker.

The spice trade port of Calcutta, 1572, the fleet preparing to sail for Europe via the Cape. An Arctic route promised a shorter and safer passage.

The Ortelius map of Europe, 1572, reveals the possibility of a northern sea route across the Russian Arctic.

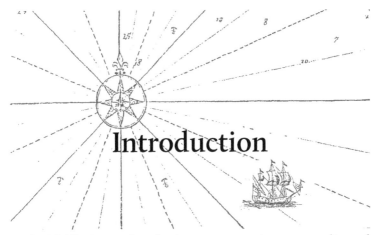

# Introduction

In the Middle Ages, oriental spices were a precious commodity and a status symbol for Europeans, but bringing them to market was costly. Overland trade routes were arduous and prey to brigands. Sea routes were long, stormy, and defended by hostile Portuguese and Spaniards.

For five centuries the British and Dutch dreamt of a trade route to Cathay (China) by way of a shortcut seaway from the Atlantic to the Pacific. Unfortunately, any northern passage lies above the Arctic Circle in one of the most severe climates on Earth: a region infested with serious ice.

Three seaways have been considered. The shortest, a crossing of the North Pole, was tried by Henry Hudson in 1607 and inevitably failed. William Parry tried and failed for the British Navy in 1827 and George De Long for the US Navy in 1879. All were frustrated by impassable ice. Yet late into the 19th century, explorers still believed that only a fringe of ice barred the way to a navigable ocean surrounding the pole.

The other two possible routes involved finding a way across the top of the continental landmass of either North America or Russia. For the Russians, Abraham Ortelius published a map in 1572 which marked a network of waterways across East Asia believing that a shipping route ran from China to a northern sea and, by way of a sea passage, to Western Europe. The native Pomors, as well as Russian settlers and traders, had been exploring the coast of the White Sea, Svalbard, Novaya Zemlya, and parts of the putative western end of the route at least as early as the 11th century. The map was roughly charted, the indigenous population well-known. This was not a situation ripe for Western European 'discovery'. It was a presumed route which needed proving.

The British struggled for four centuries to thread a northwest passage from the Davis Strait across the top of the newly discovered American continent. Disenchanted by early lack of success, they turned their attention to the possibility of the eastbound Russian route, but it was a Swedish expedition which first completed the transit.

Benefitting from Willem Barents' discoveries, Mercator's North Pole map of 1606, shows a polar rock surrounded by four islands and four rivers, but also revealing the possibility of inter-ocean navigation.

# Opening the Passage

Sir Hugh Willoughby was sent to explore a seaway to the Orient by the London-based Company of Merchant Adventurers. He sailed in 1553 with *Bona Esperanza* and *Bona Confidentia,* enduring a catastrophic voyage that ended with both crews frozen to death on the Murmansk coast. His third vessel, *Edward Bonaventure*, survived, and Willoughby's pilot, Richard Chancellor, travelled by reindeer sled to Moscow, where he met the Tsar. Ivan the Terrible treated him to epic feasts of roast swan, eaten off solid gold plates. He then sent him, complete with ship, back to London, with a letter inviting free passage and trade. The Muscovy Company was born. A fleet of sealing and whaling vessels supplied a seemingly inexhaustible bounty of Arctic wildlife products and encouraged it to think again of trade with the Far East. In 1556 the Devonian Stephen Borough

sailed with the *Edward Bonaventure* in a second attempt at the Passage. Once past the North Cape he transferred to the shallow-draft tender *Serchthrift* and surveyed the coast, reaching east to Vaigach Island before penetrating into the Kara Sea only to be defeated by 'a solid wall of ice'.

*Serchthrift*

At the end of the 16th century it was the Dutch who were most diligently investigating the possibility of an economic sea passage to the Pacific. The most notable was the 1596 expedition led by the great navigator Willem Barents, who discovered Bear Island and Svalbard. Yet this, his third attempt at a northeast passage, ended in disaster. With his vessel *Mercury* ice-bound on the northeast coast of Novaya Zemlya, his crew built a hut on the shore and survived the harsh winter on a diet of ship's  stores augmented by the foxes and bears which they trapped or shot. Building two small boats from lumber, they contrived to escape in the spring thaw. Barents perished before his crew were rescued and returned to Amsterdam. (Four centuries later, the Murman Sea was renamed the Barents Sea.)

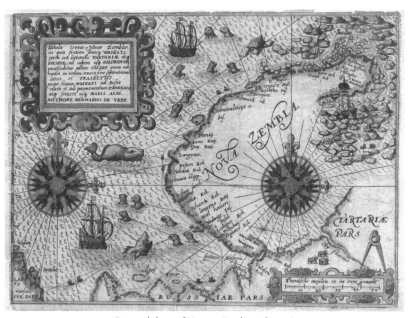

Barents' chart of Novaya Zemlya, July 1596

By the beginning of the 17th century, indigenous Pomor traders had established a sea route from Archangel to the Yamal Peninsula, using *kochs*, two-masted, skin-planked boats designed to work in light pack ice, coasting from one river mouth to another. Known as the Mangazeya Seaway, after its eastern terminus, this was an early precursor to the Russian-promoted Northern Sea Route. But Russians were suspicious of English and Dutch penetration into Siberia and denied access in 1619.

In the most famous of Cossack expeditions, Semyon Dezhnev sailed east in 1648 from the mouth of the Kolyma River to the Pacific, rounding the Chukchi Peninsula and incidentally proving that there was no land bridge from Asia to North America (though it was many years before his evidence became public).

It is possible that the Portuguese navigator David Melgueiro made the first transit of what we now call the Northeast Passage, westbound, in 1660. Sailing in the *Pai Eterno - Eternal Father*, out of Kagoshima in Japan to Porto in Portugal through the 'Arctic Ocean', Melgueiro would have taken advantage of the fact that the immediately preceding years were the warmest in almost two centuries. But conditions were normally hostile and progress in opening the passage to navigation was slow. Conditions north of the Taimyr Peninsula have always proved difficult because of compacted ice.

Tsar Peter the Great, who had spent useful time in Dutch shipyards, had grand maritime ambitions. He wanted to know the extent of his dominion and ordered the Great Northern Expedition, which struggled to map the northern coast of his empire from 1725. Much of the work was land-based but Danish-born Vitus Bering was ordered to sail north from Kamchatka. He discovered Big Diomede Island and charted the Bering Strait. It was not until May 1742 that Semyon Chelyuskin of the Russian Imperial Navy penetrated further west and reached the Cape named after him, the northernmost point of both the Northeast Passage and the Eurasian continent.

Tsar Peter the Great

By the early 19th century Norwegian fishermen and sealers were commonly working the waters of Novaya Zemlya and the Kara Sea, but the first Briton to show a practical interest was Captain Joseph Wiggins, a firm believer in the possibilities of seagoing trade. The offer of maps and promise of a trial cargo from a Russian businessman encouraged him to buy the steamer *Thames*, 120 tons. Sailing

SS *Thames*

with a cargo of sample goods from his home port of Sunderland on 8 July 1876 he crossed the Kara Sea to the lower reaches of the Yenisei river in September. Too late to risk returning with a cargo of graphite and grain, the vessel overwintered. In the spring thaw of early July 1877, she came to grief on sandbanks near the village of Goroshikha *beached beyond recovery, wrecked on our homeward track...a severe blow.*

Captain Wiggins in seagoing rig

Shoregoing splendour

Undeterred, Wiggins found backers for a new attempt. In the steamship *Warkworth*, 650 tons, he cleared Liverpool on the first of August 1878 with a cargo of general goods including porcelain, glass, salt etc., bound for Nadim on the Obi river. Picking up a return cargo of high-quality wheat, timber and furs, he was back in London on 2 October, a round trip of just two months. This promising success was sadly followed by ill-advised ventures, contributing to a distinct lack of enthusiasm for more regular commerce over the following years.

But in 1887 the *Phoenix*, 273 tons, out of South Shields 5 August, carried a cargo of salt to Yenesiesk on 9 October.

Now came Higgins's triumph. The Russian Government telegraphed to ask if he could transport 2,000 tons of rails to the Yenisei

for the proposed Trans Siberian Railway. Wiggins chartered the 2,500 ton *Orestes* and loaded 1600 tons of rails at Middlesborough. A wealthy yachtsman, Francis Leyborne-Popham, offered Wiggins command of his steam yacht *Blencathra*

*Blencathra*

as escort. He sailed from Appledore on 25 July 1893 and the flotilla, including four vessels of the Russian Navy, gathered at Vardø on 7 August. Crossing the Kara Sea without incident they reached Golchika 3 September. Barges and the smaller Russian vessels carried the rails and gold-mining equipment upriver to reach Yeneseisk on 23 October. Festivities concluded with presentation of the Emperor

Alexander III's gift of a solid silver punch bowl and mugs to Wiggins, a lifelong teetotal.

The wreck of *Thames*, lying in shallow water, was discovered by a Russian expedition in 2016 and there is talk of raising her.

## First confirmed transit

It was another hundred years before a complete passage of the trading seaway was achieved. After a series of geological expeditions in Spitsbergen, the distinguished naturalist Adolf Erik Nordenskiöld commanded an eastbound expedition of the Swedish Royal Navy, the project including an exhaustive programme of scientific research. Sailing

from Karlskrona in June 1878, the ex-whaler *Vega* entered the Kara Sea on 1 August, reaching the mouth of the Yenisei on the 6th.

Rounding the age-old challenge of Cape Chelyuskin on the 20th, they were beset in the Chukchi ice 27 September at Kolyuchin Bay. Forced to endure a winter they erected a tent over the foreparts of the vessel and allowed a protective sheet of ice to build up. *A state-*

Ice-bound *Vega*

*ly ice stair was carried up from the ice to the starboard gunwhale.*

Finally released on 18 July 1879 they passed Cape Dezhnev on the 20th before emerging triumphant into the Bering Strait and the Bering Sea. (In crossing the strait they showed conclusively for the first time that there was no land bridge between Asia and North America.)

Having successfully transited from the Atlantic to the Pacific they returned home by way of Japan, Suez and the Mediterranean, completing the voyage in the summer of 1880. In Stockholm, Nordenskiöld was elected to the Swedish Academy. King Oscar made him a baron and commander of the Order of the Polar Star.

Conquered, the Northeast Passage involved seven seas and seven time zones. But it was still a long way from being a viable commercial waterway.

Adolf Erik Nordenskiöld

The 1200 ton icebreaker *Vaygach* leaving St Petersburg
on delivery passage 1909.

Sailing from Vladivostock in the autumn of 1910 Boris Vilkitsky took command of coal-fired steam icebreakers *Taimyr* and *Vaygach*. They were destined to spend five years surveying and charting the Northern Passage pioneered by Nordenskiöld. In 1911 they made the first landing on Wrangel Island. In 1913 they discovered an archipelago which they named Nicholas II Land (now Severnaya Zemlya). In these first years, they returned to overwinter in Vladivostock. But in 1914 they set out on a westbound transit, overwintering in the Vilkitsky Strait. In finally crossing the Kara Sea and reaching Archangel in 1915, the Imperial Russian Navy's Arctic Ocean Hydrographic Expedition had succeeded in the first serious charting of the northern passage.

After the Russian Revolution of 1917, the Soviet Union found this newly-established Northern Sea Route *Severnyy Morskoy* a vital asset. As the shortest seaway between the outer limits of the immense territory, it ran completely inside Soviet waters. The arrival of radio, steam and icebreakers vastly improved the prospects of the infant route. By 1935 it had been declared open to domestic commercial exploitation. Mainland ports strengthened the infrastructure.

It was not until 1971 that the Northern Sea Route was formally opened to international shipping. Defined as running from the Kara Sea to the Bering Strait it is entirely within Russia's Exclusive Economic Zone and thus represents only a part of the Atlantic/Pacific Northeast Passage. Clearance is available at ports from Murmansk to Providenya. It is possible to transit in as little as two weeks, but since the central section is reliably free of ice for only two summer months, there is very often the expense of escort and an 'icebreaker fee'. And there is bureaucracy. Traffic remains largely Russian.

After the political breakup of the Soviet Union in the early 1990s, commercial navigation in the Siberian Arctic declined somewhat. Yet by then the route was enhanced by immensely powerful nuclear icebreakers freeing passage for conventional vessels. Regular shipping was found only from Murmansk to Dudinka in the west and between Pevek and Vladivostok in the east. Ports between Dudinka and Pevek saw virtually no shipping. Non-Russian shipping was slow to take advantage of the undoubted benefits of the shortcut from the West to Asia, saving as much as 15 days on a voyage.

The nuclear icebreaker *Sovetsky Soyuz* can lead a convoy of ten ships through the Northern Sea Route at an average speed of five knots. The ice pilot looks for leads from its helicopter.

In 1997 the Finnish tanker *Uikku* was chartered by the European Union to test the potential of year-round traffic on the Northern Sea Route. Sailing from Murmansk to the Bering Strait, she became the first Western ship to complete the voyage since Nordenskiöld in 1878.

In the early 2000s Arctic sea ice began to retreat. The Bremen-based Beluga Group claimed in 2009 that they were the first western company to make the transit without assistance from icebreakers, cutting 4,000 nautical miles off the journey between Northeast Asia and Rotterdam.

Six ships transited in 2010, 46 in 2012, 71 in 2013, 18 in 2015 and 19 in 2016. Many of them were Russian-flagged, high-capacity freighters destined for ports in China or South Korea, enjoying considerable savings in fuel. In view of the sensitive environment, research is currently exploring the possibility of replacing standard heavy fuel oil in favour of the ultra-low-sulphur version. There is also the possible future use of liquid natural gas or hydrogen systems. The International Maritime Organisation (IMO) is laying the groundwork to ban ships from using or carrying heavy fuel oil in the Arctic. But Russian approval will be necessary. Both China and Russia are investing tens of billions of dollars in expanding shipping activity in the region. At present traffic pales by comparison with that on the conventional Suez route, yet there is room for increase. In December 2015, a month after the usual end of the shipping season in mid November, the icebreaker *Vaygach* completed transit of the Northern Sea Route in a record seven and a half days. Escort icebreakers may operate in winter temperatures down to -50°C. They have 45 mm steel hulls where the 'ice skirt' meets ice and can break it working ahead or astern. First-year ice succumbs to a steady speed but pressure ridges only give way to repeated ramming. Arktika-class nuclear icebreakers are capable of breaking up to 2.5m of ice, keeping the route open for commercial traffic throughout the year. Although there is scepticism about commercial potential, retreating ice and increasingly powerful icebreakers greatly improves prospects for Pacific traffic to Western Europe. Even more intriguingly, climate change opens the prospect of a Trans-polar Passage.

The 21st century Arktika-class Russian icebreaker *50 years of victory*.

## Expedition vessels and yachts

Adventurous expedition vessels have explored Franz Josef Land but small ship and yacht voyages deeper into the Siberian Arctic remain full of potential. Permissions are not easy to organise, ice is often a problem, and infrastructure is minimal, but the islands are glorious havens of wildlife and magnificent scenery. It is prudent to attempt the passage as early as possible in the year when the ice begins to ease and the wildlife is at its best, late June to August.

Frenchman Eric Brossier made the first passage by modern sailboat in the cutter *Vagabond* in the summer of 2002, returning to France the following summer by the North**west** Passage! In the summer of 2005 the MY *Maria II* transited. In 2009 two yachts succeeded. One of them, the 36ft Norwegian sloop *RX II*, was arrested on reaching the Bering Strait for not having the correct permits. In 2010 the 60ft sloop *Peter*

*RX II*

*the First* was first to transit both Northeast and Northwest Passages in a single season, with no ice-breaker assistance.

In 2015 the Chinese trimaran *Qingdao China* set a speed record by sailing from Murmansk to the Bering Strait in 13 days. Then in 2016, in David Hempleman-Adams's Polar Ocean Challenge, the 49ft aluminium sloop *Northabout* (skipper Nilolai Litau) circumnavigated the entire Arctic Ocean, including both Northwest and Northeast Passages, in four months and a day of the summer season.

Chartered research vessels like RV *Professor Khromov* are ideal for adventurous exploration.

## Governance

The governance of the Northeast Passage has devolved to the United Nations Convention on the Law of the Sea (UNCLOS), the Arctic Council (AC), the International Maritime Organization (IMO), and the domestic legislation of the Russian Federation. In combination, they cover territorial claims, economic exploitation, technical shipping requirements, environmental protection, and search and rescue responsibilities.

The fact remains that the Northern Sea Route, that ice-choked shipping lane, is the shortest practical connection between Western Europe and Northeast Asia. Taking this alternative to the Suez Canal cuts thousands of sea miles—as much as a third of the journey.

Today, the North**West** Passage is a working waterway in summer for tourist vessels and local traffic, but its commercial potential is severely limited to the window of opportunity when the ice recedes and by the lack of infrastructure. By contrast, parts of the North**East** Passage remain ice-free all year round. The Northern Sea Route part of that passage is open to high-volume freight traffic twelve months of the year, a situation made possible by a fleet of powerful icebreakers, shore-based infrastructure and mariners with unrivalled ice experience. Only politics and bureaucracy stand in the way of increased commercial traffic and the expansion of tourism amid the scenery and wildlife-rich islands of the Siberian Arctic.

In 2016, MV *Gretke Oldendorf* carried coal from Vancouver to Raahe in Finland by way of the Northern Sea Route, making the passage twelve days faster than using the Panama Canal and saving 250mt of fuel.

Northern fulmars are common in the Chukchi and Barents Sea. Ship-followers, sometimes in large flocks, they swoop down to pick plankton thrown up in the wake. Dark plumage is characteristic of the High Arctic population.

Northern gannet colonies are well established on the Norwegian coast, range expansion could see colonisation further north. Already, fishing parties penetrate well into the Barents Sea.

# The Passage Today

## BARENTS SEA
### *Barentsevo More*

The Barents Sea links the North Sea to the Kara Sea, with Franz Josef Land and Novaya Zemlya as its eastern limit. Cold Arctic water enters from the north to form a Polar Front which has unpredictable year-on-year effects on the eastern area while the North Atlantic Drift benefits its southern half, including the port of Murmansk, which is ice-free year round.

A shallow shelf sea, it has an average depth of 230 metres, supporting a rich biological diversity of seabirds, marine mammals, and seafloor communities. Commercial fishery is hugely important, but is currently threatened by pollution, as well as oil and gas development.

Atlantic cod, key indicator of the health of the Barents Sea

## Franz Josef Land
### Zemlya Frantsa-Iosifa

Although probably first seen by Norwegian sealers, the Franz Josef Land archipelago was formally discovered on the earliest recorded landing by the Austro-Hungarian Expedition, when their vessel *Admiral Tegetthoff* was beset in drifting ice in 1873. Subsequently the 192 islands were much visited by explorers who used it as a base for North Pole expeditions, none of which succeeded.

A British flag was raised in 1925, but this was an unauthorised private venture. Norwegian sealing and hunting expeditions encouraged an ineffective attempt to assert Norwegian sovereignty in 1929. The Soviet Union had already formally annexed this northernmost territory in 1926 and Russia maintains polar stations with meteorological observatories and military bases.

The basaltic islands tend to be distinctively plateau-shaped. Glaciers are everywhere. There are plenty of Arctic foxes, but no lemmings, and therefore no snowy owls. Nevertheless, 51 bird species are recorded, 18 of which breed. There are abundant seabird cities of auks and gulls. Polar bears are common. Walrus haulouts are impressive. Other marine mammals include right, beluga, blue, and narwhal whales. Bowhead whales, whose population is endangered, are sometimes seen in these waters. A concentration of nearly 120 was seen in 2015 in the Fram Strait, west of Svalbard.

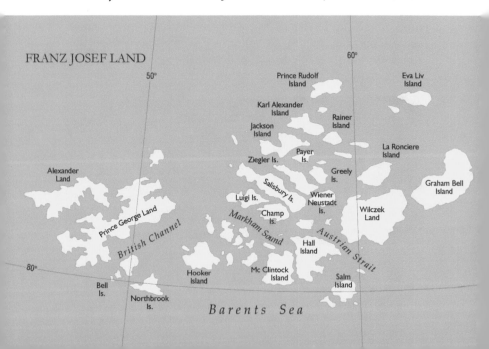

**Walrus** are creatures of the ice, living on substantial floes in the moving pack ice. The huge body is topped by a small head with small eyes. They have poor eyesight, but excellent hearing and smell. There has been much controversy in the past about the function of the remarkable upper canine teeth—the tusks. They are clearly weapons for fighting and defence. In repose they lean on them. They are certainly useful tools when the animal is hauling itself up on to an ice floe.

A walrus hunts mainly in shallow water, diving for several minutes at a time. The tusks may be used to drag it over the bottom, but it is the stiff facial whiskers that feel for the hidden clams. Powerful lips suck out the muscle and siphon, then spit out the shell. Other invertebrates and small fish are eaten whole, and it seems that they ingest a lot of gritty sand which is duly dispatched from each end, with much belching and farting. When hunters kill a walrus during the summer months they cut out the stomach, packed with its thousands of clams, and bury it until winter, when it is retrieved as a delicacy.

They are highly vulnerable to human disturbance. It is prudent to avoid getting too close, especially in a small boat, since they may attack or attempt to climb aboard.

## ALEXANDER LAND *Zemlya Karla-Aleksandry*
## 80°40′N 47°00′E

The most westerly island of the archipelago, Alexander Land, is the site of the recently established headquarters of the Russian Arctic National Park. Declared in 2009, the archipelago of Franz Josef Land and the northern part of Novaya

Nagurskoye

Zemlya represent the largest marine protected area in the Arctic.

A clandestine German meteorological station, Schatzgräber, was

St Nicholas church

established during the Second World War, but evacuated in a medical emergency by the Luftwaffe in 1944 from what became the site of the settlement and airport at Nagurskoye. This most important airport in the archipelago also serves the military Arctic Trefoil complex, monitoring Russian air space.

## BELL ISLAND *Ostrov Bell*
## 80°01′N 49°15′E

Mostly ice-free in summer, Bell Island is an idyllic place. It is home to the remains of Eira House, the earliest hut to be built in the archipelago by one of the first British explorers to penetrate the hostile Arctic ice of Franz Josef Land. Benjamin Leigh-Smith brought his expedition here in August 1880 in the auxiliary steamship *Eira*.

They had only a few nights ashore before repositioning the ship to Northbrook Island, promptly losing her off Cape Flora.

The island is a favourite venue for expeditions. The Jackson-Harmsworth Expedition made its main base here while surveying in 1894. Cape Bruce, at 80°55′N, commemorates one of Jackson's crew, William Spiers Bruce, the Scottish zoologist and oceanographer who later found distinction in the Antarctic, where he established the first weather station.

There may be bowheads in these waters, there will be terns and skuas ashore, possibly polar bears. Extensive shingle spits are close-carpeted with lichens, mosses, and a typically sparse showing of flowering plants.

Mountain avens is common in the Arctic, typical of glaciated limestone outcrops.

## NORTHBROOK ISLAND *Ostrov Nortbruka* 79°57′N 50°06′E

Northbrook Island was named after the eponymous Earl, an ex-president of the Royal Geographical Society, having served as a base for Arctic expeditions in the late 19th and early 20th centuries. The most convenient landing is at the southern end of the island, Cape Flora. Katabatic winds from the plateau may make helicopter operations difficult.

Crustose lichen

25

**Polar bears** are solitary by nature, living perhaps the loneliest life on the planet. The only time both sexes meet is during the spring courtship. After copulation the male takes no further part in family life. Helplessly weak cubs are born in a snow den in late December, blind and almost naked, but their diet of rich milk—30% fat—means that by the time the mother breaks free of the den in April the cubs are plump. At this time, conveniently, newborn ringed seal pups are at their most abundant and vulnerable. Main prey species are ringed and bearded seals, taken when the bear's sense of smell leads it to a breathing hole where it waits for prey to surface. The other main hunting technique is 'creep-and-rush'. Pursuit, whether over land or ice or sea tends to be less successful.

Summer is the lean time for polar bears. Deprived of the fast-ice with its breeding population of seals, they come ashore to snooze the time away on tundra meadows, eating eider ducks and chicks, grazing the sparse vegetation and searching for ripe berries. Amazingly, they will approach near-vertical cliffs to raid seabird colonies for eggs and chicks. At this time they are hungry and dangerous. In addition to deterrents which go bang, shore excursions need to be accompanied by a competent guard, armed with large-calibre hunting rifles or shotguns firing 12-gauge rifled slugs—used only as a last resort. The polar bear population is in decline: strict laws protect them and hunting is tightly controlled.

The **ringed seal** is the smallest and most abundant of the Arctic seals. Its dark grey back is marked with grey-white rings; the underparts generally an unspotted silver. It is shy, with good reason, since it is the favoured prey of polar bears.

Pregnant females dig a den in the fast-ice or in deep snow, its main function to give the pup a relatively warm place in which to fatten, since foxes and bears are capable of smelling them at a distance. The pup is born in late April or May, with a white woolly coat. Unusually for seals, it is not weaned for as much as two months, by which time the natal coat has been shed for its first swimming suit of silver.

Ringed seals maintain a year-round breathing hole, scratching with sharp claws through as much as 2m of solid ice. They feed on marine invertebrates and under-ice fauna, mainly crustaceans and polar cod. They suffer much from hunters but the life span can be as much as 15 or 20 years. Killer whales take some, but the main predator is the polar bear.

Cape Flora, Northbrook Island

The ground below the sheer basalt cliffs slopes down to the sea with a profuse covering of mosses and lichens, interspersed with Arctic poppies and blooming saxifrages. These richly green lower slopes benefit from the droppings of some tens of thousands of Brünnich's guillemots and black-legged kittiwakes which crowd the ledges above. Parties of snow buntings, 'Arctic sparrows', forage for seeds amongst the ground-hugging plants.

It is one of the most important historical sites in the Arctic. Just off the coast, Benjamin Leigh-Smith's vessel was crushed by ice on 21 August 1881, and his expedition took refuge ashore. In 'Eira House', a small hut made of local stone, twenty-five men (and one dog, a kitten and canary) spent the winter. They survived 10 months on ship's stores, supplemented by walrus and bear meat, before setting off (joined by a bear destined for London Zoo) in ship's boats in June 1882. Sailing towards Novaya Zemlya, they were rescued by the British vessels *Kara* and *Hope*. The wreck's position was confirmed by sonar and artifacts in Russian expeditions of summer 2017 and 2018, lying in 60 feet of water south of the island.

The Jackson-Harmsworth Expedition of 1894–1897, which completed the survey of Franz Josef Land, had a sub-base here—not

Loss of *Eira*

far from Leigh-Smith's hut. Remains of the seven buildings may still be seen. Led by Frederick Jackson, the Expedition in the steamship *Windward* was sponsored by the Royal Geographical Society. During three overwinterings at Cape Flora they discovered coal which served as fuel while undertaking meteorological, magnetic and tidal observations. Surveying the western portion of the archipelago resulted in British names for many islands, capes and bays.

The most noteworthy event of that expedition was the unexpected meeting here between the travel-worn Fridtjof Nansen and the impeccably dressed Frederick Jackson on 17 June 1896 (see pp143-6). A post was erected in 1996 to commemorate the historic occasion. (Jackson's account of the expedition *A Thousand Days in the Arctic* was published in 1899.)

There is also a small hut serving the naturalists and archaeologists of the Russian Arctic National Park.

Brünnich's guillemot

**Brünnich's guillemots** are the most northerly and the most ice-dependent of the guillemots, hugely represented along the Northeast Passage. They have a curious white stripe on the cutting edge of the mandible. Like all auks, they stand upright in penguin style. Unenthusiastic flyers, they are expert divers and underwater swimmers. Diet is almost exclusively small fish, capelin, juvenile cod, sandlance and squid, taken in dives which may reach 100m.

There are relatively few colonies, but they involve staggering numbers, sometimes well over a million birds. Guillemot 'bazaars' are sited on exposed cliffs, where the birds occupy vertiginous ledges against the rock wall, protected from the depredations of polar bears and Arctic foxes by sheer inaccessibility. Nevertheless, they have been taken in enormous numbers for their meat, perhaps half a million birds a year. At one time there was even a market for canned guillemot. The eggs, which are larger than hen's eggs, are much prized. In Novaya Zemlya, where in the 1940's and 50's some 150,000 were collected annually, they were salted for the market. After gross over-exploitation they are mostly now protected, at least on paper.

A single egg is laid on the bare ledge after the snow has melted in May or June. Fledging takes the best part of six weeks, but, amazingly, as with the common guillemot, the chick leaves the nest ledge when it is only half-fledged. Half-flying and half-fluttering, it launches itself in a perilous fall to its male parent in the sea below.

**Black-legged kittiwakes** are colonial nesters, from a couple of dozen pairs to a seabird city of thousands, often in the company of Brünnich's guillemots. They build cantilevered nests, sometimes on the narrowest ledges of very steep sea-cliffs and caves, places which offer maximum protection from marauding foxes and bears. The newly-hatched chicks are programmed to sit still, for if they were to walk about they would be in danger of falling from a great height to a certain death. They defecate over the edge of the nest, creating conspicuous white patches which encourages a healthy growth of scurvy-grass.

An ocean-going gull, in the breeding season the kittiwake's range extends as far north as there is open water for fishing. The flight is buoyant and bounding, with a shallow wing beat. There are no white tips to the wings, whose ends are 'dipped in ink'. They have a pleasant onomatopoeic call, 'kitty-wa-ake'.

Kittiwakes take a variety of food, from fish, shrimps, and marine snails to terrestrial plants and seeds. Typically, they cluster in large numbers near the snouts of glaciers, where a constant run-off of fresh water collides with the slightly warmer sea. The result is accelerated plankton production. When great chunks of ice calve from the snout, clouds of kittiwakes gather at the disturbed water to pick off the tiny crustaceans which crowd the surface.

They winter in both the North Atlantic and Pacific, foraging far out at sea.

## HOOKER ISLAND *Ostrov Gukera*
## 80°15′N 53°10′E

Hooker Island was named after Sir Joseph Dalton Hooker, botanist with James Clark Ross in the *Erebus* and *Terror* Antarctic expedition of 1839. The coast is characterised by ice cliffs rising to 400m. The highest point at 576m is the southwestern ice dome *Kupol Dzhensona*. On the western side a convenient anchorage at Calm Bay, unencumbered by glaciers, was the site of a major base for polar expeditions.

## Calm Bay *Tikhaya Buchta*
## 80°20′N 52°48′E

The bay was the site of the first Soviet Polar Station in the archipelago, established in 1929. During the Second World War the station staff were marooned. Despite a scarcity of food and general stores they maintained meteorological records and transmitted data until 1945. The station was finally abandoned in 1963, having been very much a part of the 1957/1958 International Geophysical Year. There remained a collection of clapboard huts, surrounded by the detritus wrought by decades of hard weather. Lead acid batteries, wire cable, oil drums, wooden barrels and coal dumps decorate the landscape. Birch logs wait patiently to fuel a brisk fire in a cabin stove.

A restoration of various buildings and a decontamination programme began in 2012 and much junk has been removed. The station looks a great deal smarter today. There are trails to follow; buildings have descriptive plaques revealing their former use. Occasional summer parties, mainly biologists, use the intact buildings.

The Arctic National Park Authority maintains a summer base including a small souvenir shop and a post office that accepts roubles, dollars and euros.

The ground under foot can be treacherous with mud. But there will be skuas and terns; snow and Lap-

Dog kennels at Sedov station

land buntings bring some colour. On higher ground near the site of the station are three graves: Ivan A. Zander, from Sedov's expedition; the aviator Nikolay Leske, marked by an aircraft propeller, and Piotr Fotiev, a meteorologist. Memorials commemorate Georgiy Sedov's expedition with *Svyatoy Foka* which wintered in Calm Bay in 1913–1914 on the first Russian attempt to reach the North Pole. It ended tragically in February 1914 when Sedov headed north by dog sledge, only to die of scurvy and to be buried at Cape Auk on Rudolf Island. Winter dens of polar bears have been seen on snow slopes to the north-east. Little auks numbering in the thousands nest in the boulders and rubble above a small lake.

## Rubini Rock *Skala Rubini*

Lying off Calm Bay, Rubini Rock is a volcanic plug with impressive red basalt columns rising to 82m. It was named by Frederick Jackson after Giovanni Rubini, an Italian opera singer who was said to sing as loudly as the chorus of seabirds on the near-vertical cliffs.

These are the most spectacular bird cliffs in the archipelago. Since 1931 population studies have charted the fortunes of many thousands of Brünnich's guillemots and black-legged kittiwakes. In fair conditions a ship may approach the exposed seabird city and its busy ledges almost close enough to touch and hang in the calm. The air will be noisy with the operatic murmurings of guillemots

**Harsh Arctic** conditions support few plants, but the ones that do thrive are marvels of adaptability, able to withstand biting cold, long periods without light, and the ravages of man and beast. That they survive at all is a wonder. Yet with soil just a few centimetres deep, they spread far and wide.

Mosses and lichens abound; moss campion looks like a mossy green cushion with tiny, pink five-petal flowers on very short stems. Lichens are plentiful, rock tripe is one of more than 15,000 different species. Although lichen looks like one plant it is composed of two—algae and fungi in a symbiotic relationship. They do not need soil to grow and can manage on rocks. The few flowering plants are ground-huggers. Arctic Poppy is one of the very few which can be found almost any-where along the Northeast Passage.

Rock tripe

Arctic poppy

**Little auks**, or dovekies, are the most Arctic of the auk family, with populations of millions in the Franz Josef Land and Novaya Zemlya regions of the Barents Sea. They are highly gregarious birds, indulging in mass aerobatics, almost darkening the sky, before coming ashore to their nesting area. Disturbed by an intruder or a piratical gull, they erupt as a dense flock in a 'dread'. The resulting showers of faeces fertilise a luxurious growth of lichens and mosses.

First to arrive in spring, abundant only at the western end of the Northeast Passage, they are sociable and garrulous, gathering in frost-shattered scree slopes or fissured cliffs, from sea level up to a few hundred metres.

The breeding season is timed to coincide with the seasonal peak of plankton and small fish. Specialising in taking copepods, amphipods, and other small items from the plentiful zooplankton of midsummer, they carry the catch back to the chick in a throat pouch. On emerging from the safety and darkness of the underground nest, many chicks are taken by glaucous gulls or foxes.

In autumn little auks move south. Occasionally they are driven ashore by storms and become 'wrecked', sometimes in large numbers. Settlements far from the sea may be invaded by these tiny birds walking the streets, dazed by the lights—a bizarre sight.

Red basalt columns

and onomatopoeic kittiwake calls. Below the seabird ledges, piratical glaucous gulls wait for the inevitable egg or chick to fall into their clutches. From the scree slopes, clouds of little auks swarm to the sky. Bird faeces fertilise the scurvy grass vegetation on the lower slopes. There may be walrus on ice floes amongst the pack ice.

## CHAMP ISLAND *Ostrov Champa*
## 80°38'N 56°55'E

In 1905 William S. Champ brought the *Terra Nova* here to rescue the Fiala-Ziegler North Pole Expedition which had lost their ship *America* and endured two castaway years.

This is a rugged island, ice-capped and pierced by nunataks—high peaks emerging from the snow—with icy, precipitous shores. There is an unglaciated area in the southwest.

Walrus, bearded seals, and ringed seals may all be seen on the surrounding pack ice, but fast-ice may make landing by zodiac impossible. Helicopters land conveniently under the great bluff of Cape Triest *Mys Tryest*. The sheer face of the bluff is home to thousands of guillemots and kittiwakes. The fine open beach underneath is backed by snow hills and scree slopes. Arctic skuas swoop and threaten anyone approaching their nest site or chicks. Glaucous gulls lurk. Snow buntings flutter. On outcrops of bedrock there will be a carpet of mosses; purple saxifrage and Arctic poppy may be in full flower during the summer expedition season.

Purple saxifrage is the first flowering plant to bloom in spring.

Here is the geological site for the 'Devil's Marbles', spherical geodes, some smaller than ping-pong balls, some up to 3 metres in diameter! Geodes are nothing unusual, small ones are quite common in many places. The special thing about Cape Triest, on a world scale, is their almost perfect round shape and impressive size. They usually form from a core which might be a small fossil. Chemical processes and accumulation of substances within the rock cause concretions—typically being harder and heavier than the surrounding rock. Once the sedimentary rock erodes away, the geodes are set free to lie on the surface creating an other-worldly, almost surreal, landscape. Visitors have collected souvenirs illegally on the grand scale but a fascinating selection remains, including specimens which are too large and heavy to pillage.

A 'Devil's marble'

# HALL ISLAND *Ostrov Gallya*
## 80°19′N 57°59′E

Hall Island was named after American explorer Charles Francis Hall, one of the searchers for the lost John Franklin in the Northwest Passage disaster of the 1840's. It is almost completely glaciated, but

**Narwhals** are most abundant in the west Atlantic, but range by way of Greenland east to Franz Josef Land and Severnaya Zemlya, usually in small single-sex gams. Close relative of the beluga, it is one of the world's most striking animals, spawning, with its long, spiralling tusk, the myth of the unicorn. For centuries narwhals were hunted for the ivory tusks which had great value as status symbols and, in theory at least, as aphrodisiacs. Only the male sports the extended tusk, the longest yet recorded 2.7m/8.8ft. It emerges from the left side of the upper lip, spiralling clockwise, and totally straight. In fact, there are two teeth, but the second rarely erupts from the mouth. When the whale breaks the water's surface to blow, at intervals of about a minute, the tusk is revealed first, followed by a dark blotched back with no dorsal fin.

While the population appears stable, the narwhal is vulnerable to climate change because of its limited geographical range.

A strictly Arctic species, the **bearded seal** is abundant in the pack-ice of shallow waters around the coast, wherever there are leads and polynyas. Largest of the Arctic seals, their bodies are cigar-shaped, yet with a small head, adorned with a long and bushy moustache. When wet, the hairs droop, but drying in the sun the coat appears grey and the moustache perks up. The strikingly luxuriant hairs are sensory organs of touch helping to locate clams and other molluscs and some fish on the sea bed.

On the whole they are solitary animals, not gathering in sociable herds. They typically will allow a surprisingly close approach—though they tend to rest at the edge of a floe, close to the safety of water. Their main predators are polar bears and man. They are regarded by local people as an important source of meat, lamp-oil (from the blubber) and clothing. Their bones become tools, their hides are used for the soles of shoes and for the outer skins of small boats. Chewed sealskin is used for mukluks—traditional waterproof shoes.

with spectacular sea stacks and bird cliffs. The only relatively large areas free of permanent ice are at the southeastern end of the island where there is an anchorage at Hydrographer Bay *Zaliv Gidrografov*, and a landing by the impressive headland Cape Tegetthoff *Mys Tegetkhoff*. In relatively ice-free years, bears have been encountered and an occasional swift evacuation has been prudent.

The island is the site of the earliest recorded landing in the archipelago when in 1872 the Austrian government dispatched Julius von Payer and Karl Weyprecht in the Austro-Hungarian North Pole Expedition. The object was to explore a 'Great Siberian Unfrozen Sea' in pursuit of the Northeast Passage. Admiral Tegetthoff, a 200 ton schooner sheathed in iron, powered by a 100 hp engine, was the chosen vessel. Provisioned for three years, she sailed from Bremerhaven on 13 June. Hopes of finding the north of the Barents Sea ice-free proved false. Trapped by ice they drifted in the pack, and it was many months before the monotony of life in the ice-bound ship was interrupted when they reached land-fast ice at a land which they tactfully named after their Emperor Franz Josef.

In May 1874, after enduring winter, they decided to abandon the stricken vessel. Three months of hard sledging brought them to open water in 77°40'N. Taking to their boats, they reached Novaya Zemlya on 18 August, where they found Russian fishermen. Skipper Fyodor Voronin took the 'distressed Austrian seamen' on board the schooner Nikolay for the Norwegian port of Vardø. In September, 812 days from the start of the expedition, the polar explorers returned to a triumphal welcome in Vienna. The expedition had found new land and achieved a first survey of value, but failed to find an unfrozen sea.

Abandoning *Tegetthoff*

In 1898–1899, a small camp was built here by the Wellman expedition from Ohio which was searching for the lost balloonist Andrée but also planned to sledge to the North Pole. The ice defeated them. Newspaperman Walter Wellman was an airship pioneer who flew a dirigible from Svalbard as early as 1907. Remnants of his visit can be found west of the sea stacks. A memorial to the Austro-Hungarian Expedition, erected in 1995 on behalf of the Austrian Army, stands on top of a large rock 100m from the ruins of the hut. A small grotto, near sea level on a sea stack, bears a plaque and statuette of a patron saint of mariners, St Maria of the Sea.

Remains of Wellman's base camp in 2006

Like all skuas, the **Arctic skua** is polymorphic, with two colour phases, light and dark—the lighter form having a dark breast band and being more common in high latitudes. Its main distinguishing feature is the central tail streamer. They have been seen only a few miles short of the North Pole, and call at the remotest camps to beg for scraps. Smaller than the Arctic and the pomarine, they are the commonest skuas, fast piratical predators, forcing gulls and terns to throw up their fish catch.

Arctic skuas breed on barren coasts and islands. Usually found as single pairs but sometimes in loose colonies in close association with auk, kittiwake, or tern colonies since these provide abundant prey at a convenient time in the nesting cycle. They prefer a dry nest site amid swampy ground. The pair bond is strong, probably for life. Both parents care for the young until well after fledging. The young birds fly in about 4–5 weeks fed on a diet of half-fledged auks, terns, and kittiwakes. They winter in tropical and southern seas.

Arctic skua          Long-tailed skua          Pomarine skua

## JACKSON ISLAND *Ostrov Dzheksona*
## 81°17'N 56°40'E

Part of the Zichy Land subgroup, Jackson is almost entirely covered by glaciers, with isolated nunataks and ice-caps to 480m. The deeply-indented De Long Bay on the northwest shore of the island separates it into two almost even peninsulas. From the south, this bay is bounded by Cape Bystrova, named in 1963 in honour of the Russian paleontologist A.P. Bystrow.

The island played a vitally important part in the Nansen story. Fridtjof Nansen built the vessel *Fram* in the 1880's to pursue his belief that it might be possible to reach the North Pole by using the natural drift of the polar ice (see pp143-6). West of Jackson Island five rocky islets lie among reefs. Among them, Appolonova Islet *Ostrovok Apollonova* 81°11'N 58°09'E reaches to 43·5 m. At the NW end of the islet is a low pebble spit, where there may be a walrus haulout. Narwhals and belugas have been seen in this area.

## RUDOLF ISLAND *Ostrov Rudol'fa*
## 81°47'N 58°30'E

The island was first seen from the *Admiral Tegetthoff* on 30 Aug 1873 by members of the Austro-Hungarian Expedition, unable to land as they were beset in the drifting ice (before landing on Hall Island *qv*). In the following Spring, six men and three dogs returned to survey. Reaching the northernmost part of the archipelago and hoisting the Austrian flag at Cape Fligely they completed the first, rough, mapping of Franz Josef Land.

**Arctic terns** are the only terns in the High Arctic, breeding as far north as 83°N. They may arrive at the breeding area in May before the snow has melted, gathering in colonies which can involve hundreds of noisy and aggressive pairs preparing to nest in the open, on low grassy islands, tundra flats or shingle bars. Many eggs and chicks are lost to Arctic foxes and skuas. They hover to plunge-dive in the shallows for small fish like capelin. They even hover over land to pick insects off the tundra.

Towards the end of August they leave for the long-haul flight to the other end of the planet. Wintering in Antarctica, this is the longest migration of any bird, allowing them to enjoy a life of perpetual summer.

**Snow bunting,** in perfect male summer plumage. 'Arctic sparrows' or 'snowbirds', are the most abundant songbirds in high latitudes. The breeding male is unmistakable, with all-white plumage and a black back, while the female is grey-black. Well adapted to the cold, even their legs are insulated with feathers. Busy creatures, they hunt insects and seeds over the tundra, boggy marsh, pools and sandy shores. Seeds are their main food and they find an easy living around settlements. They sing their courtship song from the eminence of a boulder or hummock, sometimes from high in the sky like a skylark. Successfully paired, they choose a crevice and build a nest of grasses, moss and lichens, lined with hair and feathers. The young are cared for by both parents until they fledge and fly before they are ten days old. Even though daylight lasts the best part of 24 hours a day in the summer, Arctic passerines tend to rest for a period of inactivity around midnight, much as birds of lower latitudes roost in the darkness of night.

Snow buntings even winter in the far north, forming mobile flocks, at the mercy of a wandering gyrfalcon.

Like the snow bunting, the **Lapland bunting** is a truly Arctic bird of the open tundra and moss-heath. Strikingly marked in summer plumage, it tends to perch conspicuously on top of a rock or in settlements, on rooftops, where it may sing like a skylark in defence of its territorial patch. On the ground or along the tideline of the seashore, it runs about vigorously in search of seeds.

The Lapland bunting may join with others to form a small colony. After the breeding season they migrate south, to winter mainly in southern Russia and Ukraine.

Rudolf is almost covered by a glacier with three ice caps, 404, 487 and 439 m high. The sides mainly slope gently, particularly in the east. The coastline is little indented except for open bays on the south and west coasts. Cape Fligely, on its northern shore, is the northernmost point of Europe and Russia.

Close to the limit of permanent polar ice, sheltered Teplitz Bay has served for a number of North Pole attempts. During 1899–1900, an expedition led by Prince Luigi Amedeo, Duke of the Abruzzi, stopped in the area. The Ziegler Polar Expedition of 1903–1905, led

by Anthony Fiala, left a large hut. A weather station established here during the second International Polar Year 1932/1933 became the northernmost scientific outpost in the world. Today it is the site of an abandoned Russian station, deserted since 1994. Something of a ghost village, snowdrifts fill sheds littered with tools. Half a bottle of beer sat on a workbench when we first landed there in 1996. Walking is not easy over large stones, boulders, mud and snow. On the scree slopes there is what may be the most northerly colony of little auks. Arctic poppy and saxifrage may bloom tenaciously in the cold.

On the headland of Cape Auk is the lonely grave of Lieutenant Georgiy Sedov, marked with a wooden cross. Leading the Russian North Pole expedition of 1912–14, he died in February 1914 after leaving Franz Josef Land with two companions on a dog-sledge attempt at the Pole.

In 1977 the USSR issued a postage stamp in honour of Sedov's birth.

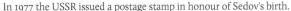

## Novaya Zemlya
### *Nova Zembla*

Novaya Zemlya, the 'New Land', is a northern extension of the Ural Mountains. There are two main islands—Northern *Severny* and Southern *Yuzhny*—separated by the narrow Matochkin Strait *Proliv Matochkin Shar*. The highest mountain, at 1547m, is located in the north. This, the larger island, represents rugged Arctic beauty at its best. There are massive extinct volcanoes, splendid glaciers and bird cliffs.

The entire archipelago may be beset by ice for much of the year, the climate severe, with frequent fog and strong winds. The vegetation in ice-free areas is predominantly low-lying grassland tundra to shrub tundra in sheltered valleys. Lemmings, Arctic foxes, reindeer, seals, walruses, and polar bears are found here. Mainland

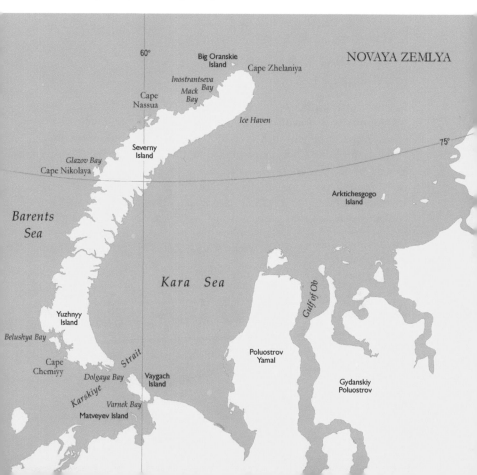

Russians knew of Novaya Zemlya from at least the 11th century, when hunters from Novgorod visited in pursuit of seals and whales. The first recorded overwintering was by Willem Barents in 1596-97.

The archipelago's recent history is largely of military significance. The administrative centre, home of the majority of the population, is in the southwest of the southern island. Beluga Bay *Guba Belushya* is in the Gusinaya Zemlya peninsula. Largely home to military personnel and their families, the town may become an oil and mining hub as Arctic shipping lanes develop.

During the Cold War the central northern region adjacent to the Matochkin Strait was a major nuclear test site. It was used for air drops and underground testing of the largest of the Soviet nuclear bombs from 1954 to 1999, including the 30 October 1961 air-burst explosion of the 54 megaton Tsar Bomba, the largest and most powerful nuclear weapon of its time. Novaya Zemlya remains a sensitive military area with restricted access.

If going for the north-about passage to the Kara Sea...

## GLAZOV BAY *Guba Glazova*
## 75°11′N 56°01′E

Barents must have coasted past, but the first recorded landing in this Admiralty Peninsula was by a Russian survey team in 1839. Another team visited with the icebreaker *Yermak* in 1901 to assess the potential for human settlement, deciding there wasn't much. There have been no permanent residents, but the scenery is magnificent; snow-capped mountains frame a stunningly beautiful glacier.

An easy landing on a driftwood-scattered pebble beach leads to an aggressive welcome from nesting Arctic terns. A tundra climb

reaches two kettle lakes and good birding: bean geese, long-tailed ducks, eiders, red-breasted mergansers, waders, and a mix of gulls.

## MACK BAY *Bukhta Maka*
## 76°23′N 64°32′E

Mack Bay is bounded by the precipitous cliffs of Cape Obrucheva, sedimentary rock tilted at a rakish angle. The Ledinik Brown glacier provides a morainal landing beach which is home for a colony of little auks which seem happy enough to pose for pictures. Behind the beach a hilly rise gradually becomes more steep to reach 1000m.

## INOSTRANTSEVA BAY *Zaliv Inostrantseva*
## 76°36′N 65°44′E

Splendid glaciers are characteristic of the west coast of Novaya Zemlya. Inostrantseva has a particularly fine one, with an uninterrupted 17 mile face. The bay offers a likely anchorage, though calving icebergs may make it uncomfortable for zodiacs. The western boundary rises to 655m.

At the tip of the northern island lies Cape Zhelaniya, with its meteorological station. In Soviet times there was a small base here that was shelled by the German Navy during World War II. In the summer of 1943 there was a clandestine Kriegsmarine seaplane base, providing German surveillance of Allied freight convoys making for Murmansk.

Cape Zhelaniya

# BIG ORANSKIE ISLAND *Ostrova Oranskie* 77°04'N 69°00'E

On this island there are well-established colonies of guillemots, little auks, kittiwakes and terns. At the extreme east of their range, Atlantic puffins bred historically on the coast of Novaya Zemlya. Mike Harris recorded the existence of a small colony in the 1950's.

**Eiders.** Common eiders are found around the coasts of Franz Josef Land, Novaya Zemlya, Wrangel Island and the Chukchi coast. Both sexes have strikingly wedge-shaped heads. The

drake is handsomely coloured, the duck is drab brown since she needs to be inconspicuous at the vulnerable ground nest. They arrive at the island breeding grounds in early spring, but

♂ common eider

wait till they are free of ice to begin nesting. The nest is a saucer of vegetation, often in the lee of a feature such as a rock or tide-line debris. It will be lined and insulated generously with down feathers pulled from the duck's own breast (the eiderdown which is much valued for its insulation properties). Gregarious birds, they nest colonially. The parental bond is weak, ducklings soon form into crèches.

**King eiders** are even more colourful, though they are often seen in drab moult towards the end of the breeding season. On a bluish-grey nape, the drake's bill is bright orange. Smaller

♀ king eider

than the common eider, less colonial, kings often choose to nest close to one other pair. Though they are not found on Franz Josef Land, they are widely distributed along the entire Northeast Passage coast.

Eiders dive in shallow water for crustaceans and molluscs, mussels for choice. Swallowed whole, the

♂ king eider

shells are crushed in the stomach. They winter at the edge of a polynya—a stretch of open water surrounded by ice.

## ICE HAVEN *Gavan Ledyanaya*
## 76°15′N 68°18′E

The Dutch navigator Willem Barents surmised that the twenty-four hours of summer sun would melt the Arctic ice and open a summer passage to the Pacific. In his third attempt at navigating the northern jigsaw and in pursuit of a handsome reward for revealing the Northeast Passage he sailed from Amsterdam in May 1596 with two ships and a cargo of trade merchandise, one under himself, the other commanded by John Rijp. Reaching the Murman (Barents) Sea in June they had encounters with polar bears.

The two ships parted, to explore both south-about and north-about in looking for the best way around Novaya Zemlya. John Rijp failed to find a south-about route and turned back for home. Barents sailed northeast to round the northern cape and find open water. But the summer season was coming to an end as he encountered serious ice when he entered the Kara Sea.

*The 26 of August there blew a reasonable gale of wind, at which time we determined to sail back home again. But the ice began to drive with such force, that we were enclosed round about therewith, and yet we sought all the means we could to get out, but it was all in vain.*

*The same day in the evening we got to the west side of the Ice Haven, where we were forced, in great cold, poverty, misery and grief, to stay all the winter: the wind then being east north-east.*

They built a driftwood hut—*het Behouden Huys*—the Safe House, surviving the horrendous cold with the help of stores from the ship complemented by fox and bear meat and skins. *...it blew hard northeast, and it froze so hard that, as we put a nail into our mouths (as, when men work carpenter's work, they use to do), there would ice hang thereon when we took it out again, and make the blood follow.*

In June the next year, with their ship still fast in the ice, they abandoned her and set sail in the ship's boats. *...committing ourselves to the will and mercy of God, with a west north-west wind and an indifferent open water, we set sail and put to sea.*

Carrying not only victuals but a fair sample of the merchant goods they were responsible for, they set out into an ice-cluttered sea on 13 June. On the 20th Barents died suddenly while in conversation with chronicler Gerrit de Veer. *The death of William Barents put us in no small discomfort, as being the chief guide and only pilot on whom we reposed ourselves next under God.*

It was seven weeks before the boats reached the Kola Peninsula and rescue by a Russian merchant vessel. Only 12 crewmen remained by the time they reached Amsterdam 1 November.

275 years later, in 1871, Norwegian Captain Elling Carlsen, on a sealing hunt in the sloop *Solid*, was first to re-visit Barents' house. It was still intact. He removed perfectly preserved relics which are now on display in the Rijksmuseum in Amsterdam.

In 1992 an expedition sent by the Arctic and Antarctic Research Institute in St. Petersburg erected a commemorative marker. Today, only shattered pieces of timber from the house remain on the beach.

If taking the south-about passage to the Kara Sea...

## VAYGACH ISLAND *Ostrov Vaygach*
## 70°03'N 59°20'E

Vaygach is a low-lying tundra island, with rivers serving bird-rich wetland. Raised beaches are evidence of its recent geological past. It is separated from Novaya Zemlya by the Kara Strait *Proliv Karskiye Vorota*, a 35 mile wide ship channel connecting the Barents to the Kara Sea.

Until the 19th century, the island was regarded as a sacred place, an important shrine of the Nenets people. There were wooden idols painted with the blood of holy animals, usually reindeer. In post-So-

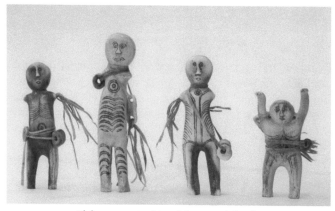

Idols represent spirits of the owner's family

viet Arctic Russia, Baptist missionaries of Russian and Ukrainian origin have been fighting against idolatry and persuading the Nenets to burn their sacred images or *khekhe*. There are still sacrificial piles of driftwood, antlers and skulls. In the past the island was the object of pilgrimage for the nomadic reindeer herders travelling by sledge and living in reindeer-hide tents. Some 40,000 reindeer summer here. Nenets (Samoyed) people are well established in the region, recognized as indigenous Siberians. Largely Orthodox Christian nowadays, there remains great respect for traditions. At its peak, Vaygach Island had a population of over 5,000, but now just over 500 remain, scattered in a handful of villages like that at Varnek Bay.

Varnek village, Vaygach Island

Reindeer are central to the social, cultural, spiritual and economic life of the Nenets people, the largest indigenous group in the Russian North. Herders enjoy a close relationship with their animals throughout the year, moving herds from the summer pastures to winter on the mainland further south. Reindeer husbandry is a thriving industry.

Archangel, circa 1900.

## Dolgaya Bay *Guba Dolgaya*
## 70°15'N 58°25'E

There is a shallow anchorage amongst bird-rich islets at the north end of the island. Above the pebbly beach there is a summer abundance of wildflowers and plant life, the Arctic in bloom. This marshy tundra is blessed with lagoons and lakes; in high summer there will be barnacle and bean geese, long-tailed ducks, common eiders, scoters and scaup at the shore. There may be Bewick's swans, divers, red-breasted mergansers and a mix of shorebirds. There may be a walrus haulout.

## MATVEYEV ISLAND *Ostrov Matveyev*
## 69°28'N 58°32'E

Just west of Varnek Bay, this island, part of the Nenets State Nature Reserve, is said to be home for a large population of Atlantic walrus. Traditionally, fishermen called here to collect eider eggs.

**Walrus** are never far from shore, especially when summer ice may be scarce. They haul out in large numbers and lie almost on top of each other, a classic example of *thigmotaxis*—'bodies in close contact'. Unfortunately for them, their tusks have cash value.

Oosik is a term used in native cultures to describe the baculum (penis bone) of seals and polar bears. The male walrus has the largest of any mammal, as much as 55cm in length. Oosiks, polished and sometimes carved, are used as handles for knives and other tools and sold to tourists as souvenirs.

# KARA SEA
## *Karskoye More*

An important waterway in the early exploration of the Northeast Passage. Originally largely unknown as the Glacial Sea, it stretches from Novaya Zemlya to Severnaya Zemlya. Mostly unexplored till the late 19th century, now named for the Kara 'North' River, its temperature is markedly colder than that of the Barents Sea since it derives no advantage from the North Atlantic Drift. Several other rivers bring fresh water contributing to variable salinity and freezing for over nine months of the year. Currents move in two slow, counterclockwise gyres in the southwestern and northeastern parts of the Sea. There are frequent gales and snowstorms in winter, while in summertime snow, snow squalls, and fog are the order of the day.

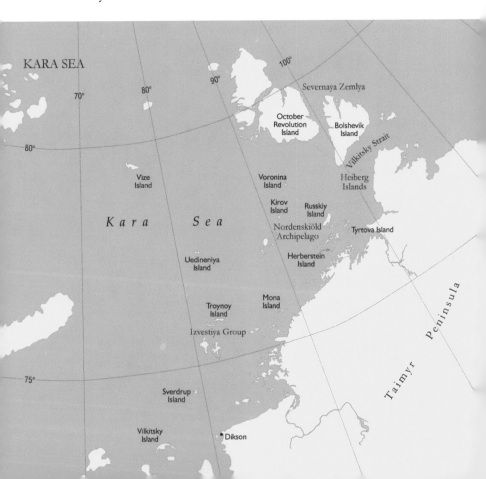

Much of the sea area and the many islands form part of the Great Arctic State Nature Reserve. With an area of 41,692 km², it is the largest Russian reserve—*zapovednik*—as well as one of the largest in the world. Divided into nine sections, it ranges from the Barents Sea to the Taimyr peninsula and includes fine examples of the biological diversity of the Siberian Arctic. Fishing for cod, salmon, and sturgeon is an important economic activity; discoveries of petroleum and natural gas are in the planning stages of development by Rosneft with Exxon.

## DIKSON
## 73°30′N 80°25′E

50 years of Dikson, 1965

Dikson is an important port on the Northern Sea Route, handling general cargoes mainly from Murmansk—130,000 tonnes in 2008. Sealing and fishery operations are important here. There is a major polar research station as well as radio and meteorological stations. There are links to the Trans-Siberian railway at Krasnoyarsk, but its population is reduced to 3,000 now that much of the military has been re-deployed.

The name comes from Baron Oscar Dickson, a wealthy Swedish Arctic explorer and one of the sponsors of both Nordenskiöld's *Vega* and Nansen's *Fram* expeditions. Dikson is one of the many settlements claiming to be the most northerly in the world.

## TROYNOY ISLAND *Ostrov Troynoi*
## 75°55′N 83°16′E

Troynoy is one of four islands, two large and two small, in the Izvestiy group (named for the famous Russian broadsheets *Pravda* and *Izvestia*). It is 27km long, gently sloping, and dome-like with numerous rock formations and ribs, rising to 42m.

Shoreline shingle and ice is littered with current-borne driftwood from the great river deltas further east. Above the beach, there is sparse tundra vegetation. There are lichens, some mosses and fungi, and only a few higher plants. Most distinctive features are the numerous ridges with erratic blocks up to three metres in

Red-throated diver with chick

diameter. One of these may be the site of a breeding colony of ivory gulls, where they sit on their little mounds of mud, decorated with moss and lichen. But ivory gulls are atypical seabirds; they often try new breeding sites.

There is plenty of bird and mammal life. Brent geese, red-throated divers, both eiders, pomarine skuas and Arctic terns. No lemmings, so no snowy owls. But reindeer, walrus, polar bears, ringed and bearded seals are here as well as beluga whales. There is a meteorological station *Polyarnaya Stantsiya*.

Current-borne driftwood, a common sight on Arctic beaches, provides valuable building material and fuel.

## UYEDINENIYA ISLAND *Ostrov Uyedineniya*
### 77°30′N 82°20′E

Norwegian explorer Edvard Holm Johannesen from Tromsø discovered this isolated island on 26 August 1878, naming it *Ensom-
heden,* Solitude. The nearest land is 150km to the south, the Izvestiy
Islands. The anchorage is off the precipitous NW coast, opposite
the polar station. The island is otherwise uninhabited.

Uyedineniya is flat and low-lying, with some swamps and small
lakes and a long pebble-spit of land on its NE. Its highest point
is only about 30m. Ice-bound throughout the winter months the
weather is bleak and severe, fast-ice is common even in the summer.

# The Nordenskiöld Archipelago

The Nordenskiöld Archipelago is a complex cluster of about 90
windswept, ice-bound, and desolate granitic islands in the eastern
region of the Kara Sea, stretching for almost 100km from west to
east and about 90km from north to south along this coastal region.
The group was first reported in 1740 by Nikifor Chekin of the Great
Northern Expedition but named much later for the much-travelled
polar explorer, by Nansen, in his charts of the Siberian coast.

The islands were mapped by Captain Fyodor Andreyevich
Matisen during the Russian Polar Expedition of 1900–1903. Matisen
twice crisscrossed the vast frozen area by dogsled. The archipelago
was explored in the 1930s by Soviet expeditions with the icebreakers
*Sedov* and *Toros.* Except for weather stations, there is no settlement
on any island of the archipelago.

## Kirov Islands, *Ostrova Sergeya Kirova*
### 77°36′N 91°55′E

The Kirov Islands are ice-bound, though with some polynyas,
through much of the year. Ice floes remain even in the summer.
This group, as well as its northernmost island, Kirova, is named after Stalin's politburo member Sergey Kirov.

The largest island is Isachenko, 168km² rising to an elevation of
55m. Its coasts are mainly precipitous, reaching 23m in the NW. The
NE of the island is low and boggy. An active polar station stands on
the SW coast.

## RUSSKIY ISLAND *Ostrov Russkiy*
## 77°03′N 96°05′E

Russkiy Island is the northernmost and largest of the Izvestiy group. In 1935, during Soviet times, a weather station was established here, the only permanently inhabited place in the whole Nordenskiöld archipelago. In addition to meteorological measurements, the purpose was to monitor Arctic navigation along the Northern Sea Route. Scientific research continued after the breakup of the Soviet Union, but the station was closed in 1999.

On the roof of the abandoned station, just north of Cape Russkiy Severny, there is a 13m lighthouse and two 25m radio masts. A freshwater lake is worth checking for birds.

It was off the NW coast of Russkiy in August 1942 that the famous icebreaker *Aleksandr Sibiryakov* faced an unequal fight with the Kriegsmarine heavy cruiser *Admiral Scheer*. In a one-hour battle—3 inch versus 11 inch guns—she went down with the loss of most of her crew. Her radio transmissions alerted convoys, giving them time to avoid the area.

## HERBERSTEIN ISLAND *Ostrov Malyy*
## 76°25′N 97°25′E

Baron Sigismund von Herberstein was the 16<sup>th</sup> century Holy Roman Emperor Maximilian's ambassador to Russia, with strong diplomatic connections to Moscow.

Herberstein Island is small, ice-bound, low-lying and rocky, the beach strewn with driftwood. Soggy tundra offers abundant woolly and red mosses, the rocky outcrops are decorated with worm, map, mane, pixie cup lichens and rock tripe. There are sedges. The only flower found on one landing was nodding saxifrage.

## TYRTOVA ISLAND *Ostrov Tyrtova*
## 76°38'N 97°28'E

The landing at the southeastern end of Tyrtova Island is low-lying and with topography similar to that of Herberstein Island—at first sight unremarkable but with a more extensive and diverse area to explore. Now uninhabited, there are remains of a 1945–75 meteorological station, complete with rusting oil drums and general detritus. Walking can be challenging, hampered by snow and ice. The higher tundra tends to be easier to negotiate. Common and king eiders, brent geese, terns, skuas and buntings are all here, plus rather more plants than on the smaller island—among them least willow, cinquefoil, nodding saxifrage and Arctic poppy.

Sheltered anchorage may also be found in the southwestern Yu-zhnaya Bay, though countercurrents may fill the bay with ice.

## HEIBERG ISLANDS *Ostrova Geyberga*
## 77°40'N 101°27'E

Financier Axel Heiberg supported the Norwegian brothers Amund and Ellef Ringnes in setting up their brewery in 1876. In due course Fridtjof Nansen honoured him as the main backer, along with shipowner Thomas Fearnley, of his vessel *Fram*, and the North Pole expedition of 1893.

The group of four small tundra islands—the largest some 5km in length—lies 25 miles from the continental shore and marks the western entrance to the Vilkitsky Strait. Ice-bound for most of the year, they are obstructed by pack ice even in the summer. A 1940 meteorological station, long abandoned, serves as a navigation daymark on the Northern Sea Route.

**Glaucous gulls** ('glaucous' is from the Greek glaukos, bright or gleaming) are big birds, larger, heavier, and paler than the familiar and similar-looking herring gull, and even more aggressive. They are often found near settlements and in association with goose grounds, kittiwake or auk colonies which provide convenient prey. They keep station with a ship on any journey in the Passage, visiting in the hope of scraps, perching fearlessly on the rails.

They are omnivorous, but in the breeding season sustain themselves mostly from the eggs and chicks of other birds. As piratical scavengers they take the eggs and young of auks and kittiwakes. Waiting below the cliff face, they take young birds as they tumble on their first perilous descent from the nest ledge, and also lie in wait for those chicks which have to

First year juvenile

run the gauntlet from the cliff base over tundra to the sea. They also rob eider and fulmar nests. Storm-tossed mussels may be taken on the beach, where they will also search for fly larvae in the tideline detritus. Seal faeces may provide some nourishment. Adult little auks are caught in flight and eaten whole.

**Ivory gulls** are slightly larger than a kittiwake. Pure white, with a stout pale-yellow bill, a red eye-ring and short black legs. A truly Arctic species, spending its whole life breeding and wintering above 70°N. The webs between their toes are much reduced, by comparison with other gulls, to minimise heat loss. Their claws are curved to improve grip on ice.

Ivory gulls are principally scavengers. They are heavily dependent on the pickings from polar bear kills, tending to keep company with the bears in order to benefit from the remains of flesh and blubber which litter the killing ground. They follow dog teams and can be found around human habitation in the hope of handouts.

First-year juvenile

Closely related to Sabine's gull, they breed in large numbers on Franz Josef Land, on islands in the Kara Sea and on Severnaya Zemlya. The colonies are sometimes on level ground, though they run the risk of being taken or trodden by polar bears. They are markedly tolerant of human presence, seeming tame and fearless. They winter along the edge of the pack ice and polynyas in the Chukchi and Bering Seas.

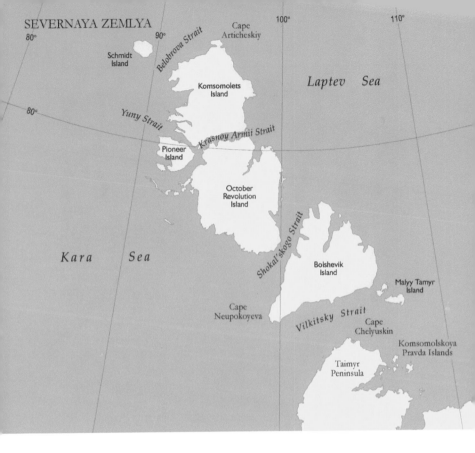

Schmidt Island

Cape Articheskiy

Belobrova Strait

Laptev Sea

Komsomolets Island

Yuny Strait

Krasnoy Armii Strait

Pioneer Island

October Revolution Island

Kara Sea

Shokal'skogo Strait

Bolshevik Island

Malyy Tamyr Island

Cape Neupokoyeva

Vilkitsky Strait

Cape Chelyuskin

Komsomolskoya Pravda Islands

Taimyr Peninsula

## Severnaya Zemlya
### *Severnaya Zemlya*

The half glaciated archipelago of Severnaya Zemlya, the 'Northern Land', separates the Kara Sea in the west from the Laptev Sea in the east. It has always been known as an area held in the grip of year-round fast-ice, with access to the southernmost island occasionally free in high summer. More recently, ice conditions have relented somewhat and there has been open water even to the north of the archipelago.

It was first discovered by Boris Vilkitsky in 1913, who presumed there was only one island. But on 15 May 1928 the archipelago was overflown and partially mapped by Umberto Nobile and his crew in the Airship *Italia*. In 1931 the

expedition of Georgy Ushakov and Nikolay Urvantsev made the first detailed map of the archipelago, showing Severnaya Zemlya to be divided into four main islands.

In 1913 Vilkitsky had called this new land Emperor Nicholas II Land *Zemlya Imperatora Nikolaya II*, but in 1926 the Presidium of the Central Executive Committee of the USSR renamed the archipelago Severnaya Zemlya. A more recent request by the Krasnoyarsk administrative region to reinstate the former name was rejected.

A comprehensive geological map was compiled in the 1940s and 1950s by a team of geologists from the Scientific Research Institute of Arctic Geology in St. Petersburg.

## BOLSHEVIK ISLAND *Ostrov Bolshevik*
## 79°00'N 102°00'E

Bolshevik is the southernmost and the second largest island of the group. Much of the island is covered by glacier systems, its mountains reaching 935m, while the coastal plains have a sparse vegetation of mosses and lichens. Its northwestern shore has some fine fjords. There is a meteorological station, Baranov, where some thirty scientists are also working on the geology, geophysics, and ice coring.

A landing on the southern coast at Sunny Bay *Bukhta Solnechnaya* (opposite the remains of the abandoned Somnitelnaya polar station) offers the chance of phalaropes feeding near the beach, plus tundra walks over a rocky surface, possibly accompanied by mosquitos. Large numbers of belugas have been seen.

**Belugas** are sociable creatures, rarely alone, relatively common around the icy coasts of the Siberian Arctic. A talkative species, they have a highly-developed sense of hearing. The whaler's term 'gam' would be the perfect collective noun for these 'sea canaries' because of their varied and musical vocabulary. They indulge in trills, clicks, squeals, bell sounds, whistles and rasp-berries, sounds which can be heard clearly above the surface. The name comes from the Russian for 'white one'.

They are slow swimmers but dive deep, hunting down to 700m for bottom fish such as halibut, capelin, char, cod, and lantern fish, or to nuzzle in the silt for invertebrates. Summer-ing to calve in the High Arctic, they migrate to winter in the Barents or Bering Seas; a few reach as far as Scotland in the Atlantic, some to Japanese waters in the Pacific. Although the species is regarded as endangered in some areas, the world population has been estimated as somewhere between 100,000 and 200,000. They may live for 30 years, possibly 40. There is currently no sign of overfishing, but in conservation terms they are classified as 'near threatened'. Easily trapped because of its dependence on breathing holes, the beluga's skin is prized for the delicacy muktuk, which is chewed raw, eaten boiled or smoked. The almost transparent blubber is used as a fuel oil for lamps.

## The Vilkitsky Strait *Proliv Vilkitskogo*

The Vilkitsky Strait, between the Taimyr Peninsula and Bolshevik Island in the Severnaya Zemlya archipelago, connects the Kara to the Laptev Sea. It is the northernmost strait and a vital link for marine traffic. Ice conditions are severely challenging here; navigation is restricted by the pack ice which is compacted in the relatively narrow waterway (55km) and further restricted by the tendency of strong currents to compress it. In this crucial part of the Northern Sea Route icebreakers are on standby throughout the navigation season to assist other vessels.

Boris Andreyevich Vilkitsky (1885–1961), hydrographer and surveyor, led the Arctic Ocean Hydrographic Expedition in 1910–15 in the icebreakers *Taimyr* and *Vaygach*, surveying for the Northern Sea Route and transiting the immensely difficult strait now named after him. On 22 August 1913, Vilkitsky sailed on to make the first Russian voyage from Vladivostok to Archangel (but not the ocean to ocean Northeast Passage, earlier claimed by Nordenskiöld).

The steam icebreakers *Taimyr* and *Vaygach*

## CAPE CHELYUSKIN *Mys Chelyuskina* 77°43'N 104°15'E

Cape Chelyuskin is the northernmost point of the Eurasian continent, 1370kms from the North Pole, gateway to the Taimyr peninsula. The rocky shore is home for the Fyodorov Hydrometeorological Observatory and a border post representing the sovereignty of the Russian Federation and handling the bureaucracy of landing permissions. It is a bleak spot, littered with oil drums and general refuse, a common problem in a region enduring permafrost. Commemorative monuments honour explorers of the past: Chelyuskin, who came here in 1742 as a member of Peter the Great's Siberian expedition; a tall column of slate celebrates Nordenskiöld, first to sail the complete Northeast Passage in *Vega*, 1878; Amundsen is remembered for his 1919 visit in *Maud*. Certainly a memorable location, redolent of centuries of heroic exploration.

## The Taimyr Peninsula

The Great Arctic State Nature Reserve, 400,000km² of islands and mainland and the largest Russian nature reserve, was inaugurated here on the Taimyr Peninsula in 1993. Some 2,000 years ago the last of the muskoxen occurring naturally outside North America died out in this region. They were successfully reintroduced with

Nordenskiöld's *Vega*, escorted by the Russian steamship *Lena*, rounded Cape Chelyuskin 19 August 1878.

Canadian stock in 1975. The 20 incomers increased to 2,500 by 2002 to 9,000 in 2012.

The indigenous people are Samoyedic, including Nenets and Nganasan. The isolated nature of the peninsula made it possible for the Ngansans to maintain their shamanistic practices in settlements like Volochanka.

Mining operations in the area produce nickel ore which is taken by rail to the port city of Dudinka on the Yenisei River and from there by sea to Murmansk.

Volochanka

## MAUD BAY *Bukhta Mod*
## 77°38'N 104°52'E

Maud Bay offers an attractive opportunity for a wilderness landing on the Taimyr Peninsula. Lying between Capes Papanina and Amundsena, some nine miles east of Cape Chelyuskin, two rivers empty into the bay at the foot of gently sloping hills, dividing it by a small rocky peninsula into two parts.. A sand spit and lagoon backed by a pebble beach leads to pleasantly walkable flat country with plenty of vegetation, spider plants being especially abundant. There will be birds but maybe polar bears.

Spider plant *Saxifraga flagellaris*

The present Northeast Passage population of **muskoxen** owes its presence to re-introductions from Nunavut in Canada in the 1970's (having abandoned Siberia to migrate across the land bridge to North America thousands of years ago).

Tough and heavily built, standing five to eight feet tall at the shoulder, they are protected from winter cold down to −50°C by a dense undercoat of woolly fur, topped by outer guard hairs which provide a skirt reaching almost to the ground. The inner fleece is known as qiviut. Finest of all wool, it can be knit-ted to make fabrics of exceptional warmth while remaining very light in weight.

In the high summer rut bulls produce the rank-smelling musk which gives the species its name. This attracts females, serves as a territorial marker and plays its part in royal battles. The herd of a dozen or so is under the control of a dominant bull during the rutting season but alpha females take over when grazing decisions become more important than procreation. Their only serious predator, apart from man, is the wolf. Un-der attack, they gather in a tight circle, enclosing the calves and lowering their heads to offer a ring of sharp horns to circling wolves: an effective defence strategy, except against guns. Approach with great care; these animals are shy, but also exceedingly dangerous, charging furiously when disturbed.

In summer, oxen feed on the vegetation of the coastal val-leys, mainly on succulent grasses and dwarf willow, building up a thick layer of fat to survive the winter.

**Reindeer** are the most northerly of all deer. Small animals, the buck reaches to about a metre at the shoulder. Both sexes have antlers, the only deer with this distinction. Ranging widely over the tundra and islands, they are slow-moving and relatively easy to approach. Their main diet is the moss *Cladonia rangiferina*, but they will also graze willow and birch and may even take lemmings and birds eggs. Chukchi herders find they enjoy the magic of mushrooms.

They have been semi-domesticated to great economic advantage through the millennia. Wild reindeer herds of a million animals exist in the Taimyr region, enormously important to indigenous people like the Nenets, providing milk and meat for their families and dogs, skins for bedding, clothing and tents, antlers for tools. A reindeer-drawn sled has the advantage over huskies that the deer find their own forage as they travel. Traditionally, nomadic herders migrate with their flocks between coast and inland areas according to an annual migration route. The arrival of high-powered rifles has encouraged overkill and may jeopardise their survival in the wild.

# LAPTEV SEA
## *More Laptevykh*

The Laptev Sea is located between Severnaya Zemlya and the New Siberian Islands.

Dmitry Laptev was a distinguished officer in the Russian Navy who served in the 1735 Kamchatka Expedition under Vitus Bering, charting the coast to the delta of the great river Lena. From about the 18th century the newly-coastal Yakut tribes were the principal fishermen (sardines, cod, and Arctic char) and hunters (seals and walrus), before the arrival of the Russians.

The sea is frozen for most of the year, open to navigation only in the August–September window, unless icebreaker-assisted. There are many islands, some containing perfectly-preserved mammoth remains frozen in the permafrost.

Coastal settlements are few and small, except for Tiksi.

## Komsomolskoya Pravda Islands
### *Ostrova Komsomol'skoy Pravdy*
### 77°30′N 107°00′E

First reported in 1736 by Russian explorer Vasili Pronchishchev, there are nine uninhabited islands 20 miles E of Cape Kharitona Lapteva. Their coasts are formed from steep sloping hills which terminate as 15 to 20m cliffs.

Samuila Island and Bol'shoy (the largest) belong to an offshore subgrouping.

Samuila 77°29′N 106°45′E, has lower regions of marshy tundra with a freshwater pond, a central saddle with rocky hills to 25m.

Smaller islands form another subgroup known as the Vilkitsky Islands (not to be confused with other Vilkitsky Islands elsewhere).

Cotton grass *Eriophorum scheuchzeri*

## TIKSI
## 71°39'N 128°48'E

The port of Tiksi, reached year-round by way of the Lena River, serves as principal access to the Laptev Sea. As the largest settlement and an important administrative centre it lies roughly halfway along the Northern Sea Route. Population 5,063 in the 2010 census.

The important meteorological station was upgraded in 2006 and has become part of the Atmospheric Observatory program of the US National Oceanic and Atmospheric Administration agency—one of four Arctic Weather Stations at the world's northernmost settlements, others are at Barrow in Alaska, Eureka and Alert in Canada's Nunavut. They collect weather information and research stewardship of the ocean environment.

Polyarka weather station, Tiksi

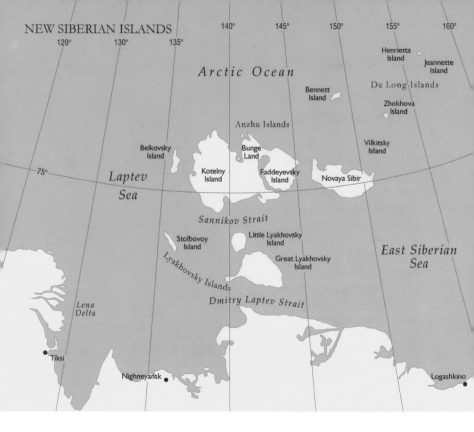

## New Siberian Islands
### *Novosibirskiye Ostrova*

This low-lying archipelago between the Laptev and East Siberian Seas is made of a mixture of folded and faulted sedimentary and igneous rocks ranging in age from Precambrian to Pliocene. The sediments, ranging in thickness from a fraction of a metre to about 35 metres, are cemented by permafrost and have accumulated over the last 200,000 years. They are remarkable for the quantity of the extinct mammoth and rhino remains they hold in a 'wonderful state of preservation'. Marine surveyor Chvoinoff first recorded them in 1775. Later visitors collected the valuable specimens energetically.

Behind pebble beaches, the landscape is predominantly tundra, with many hummocks, gorges, small rivers, lakes and marsh.

There are few sheltered anchorages. South of the islands, the pack ice in the Dmitry Laptev Strait may be compressed by strong currents to create challenging navigation conditions. Better news is that in the summer months the sun stays above the horizon.

## KOTELNY ISLAND *Ostrov Kotelnyy*
## 75°30′N 139°00′E

At 23,165 km² Kotelny is one of the largest islands in the world. When the explorer Ivan Lyakhov arrived in 1773, he is said to have found evidence of early occupation, including the copper kettle which accounts for the name.

Landing by Cape Anisiy, there is a shoreline of icy ridges of sand and gravel. Pebble beaches are littered with driftwood logs, bounty of the spring floods on the Siberian rivers. This timber has historically been invaluable on these treeless islands for fuel and the construction of trapper's huts and sledges.

Gentle hills of tundra are pierced with lemming holes while the remains of huts provide homes for yet more lemmings; there are metre-deep holes with the remains of even earlier yarangas. Everywhere there is evidence of a hunting past: reindeer and fox bones, seal jaws, a walrus skeleton, poles for drying animal skins. There are still reindeer on the island.

Kotelny is inhabited only by a thriving military base, re-established in 2014 after major decontamination of the site.

## BELKOVSKIY ISLAND *Ostrov Belkovskiy*
## 75°37′N 135°52′E

The westernmost island of the archipelago, Belkovskiy, was discovered in 1808 by a Russian fur merchant named Belkov. Shingle beaches on the lower east coast are rock-strewn and backed

Thilo Bay, Belkovskiy Island

by ponds which might have Ross's gulls dipping for larvae. There will be lemmings enjoying the holes and tunnels associated with the remains of trappers' huts and therefore the chance of a snowy owl. The least decrepit hut may still have an abandoned scale used for weighing walrus oil and dating back to the days of Mr Belkov's walrus exploitation and bear trapping.

The island's vegetation is the typical tundra of low-growing grasses, rushes, forbs, mosses, lichens, and liverworts.

From the 120m clifftop at the northern end of the island the walrus haulout on the pebble beach below can be spectacular. It has long been established that the Atlantic and Pacific walrus represent separate subspecies but the taxonomic status of these Laptev walrus has been uncertain. It has been described as intermediate in size between the Pacific and Atlantic forms, with skull morphology similar to the Pacific subspecies. One current suggestion is that the Laptev walrus should be recognized as the westernmost population of the Pacific walrus, sub-sp *laptevi*.

Laptev walrus are a possible sub-species which exist in the centre of the world walrus range, midway between the relatively short-tusked Atlantic and the long-tusked Pacific form. Polar bears treat them with hungry respect.

The Arctic willow survives in this challenging habitat by virtue of being small and stunted, barely ankle-high. Adapted to the permafrost, with shallow roots, it may cover the ground like a carpet. Other trees, pine and birch, exist in the region, but they are always dwarfed and extremely sparse.

## Lyakhovsky Islands *Ostrova Lyakhovskiye* 73°40′N 140°00′E

This southernmost group of the New Siberian Islands was first explored by Ivan Lyakhov in 1773. They are separated from the mainland by the 6okm Laptev Strait. Two islands dominate the group.

Great, or Bolshoy, Lyakhovsky, is the largest with an area of 4,600 km² and a maximum altitude of 270m, consisting of highly folded and faulted Precambrian metamorphic rocks. The vegetation is a mixture of tundra and wetland dominated by sedges, grasses, and mosses.

In the early 19th century Yakov Sannikov had reported the sighting of a 'new land' north of Kotelny. 'Sannikov Land' bewitched explorers, including Baron Eduard von Toll who dog-sledged in the area in 1892. He never found the non-existent *Zemlya Sannikova* but landed on Great Lyakhovsky and was one of the first to confirm the existence of mammoth bones and significant quantities of

Pleistocene fossil ivory in the frozen sediments of beaches and river beds. Radiocarbon dating has shown that the ivory accumulated on this and other New Siberian islands over a period of some 200,000 years. In 2014, researchers discovered a paleolithic spear tip formed from woolly rhino horn, dated 13,300 years old.

The Cape Shalaurova meteorological station, named for merchant explorer Nikita Shalaurov, lies on the southeast coast of the island and provides climatic data for this island. The mean precipitation is 184 mm/year. The heaviest, about two-thirds of the yearly total, occurs between June and September. August is the warmest month with a mean temperature of 2.4°C.

Little Lyakhovsky is the second largest of the group, with an area of 1,325km². Tundra covers most of the island—low-growing grasses, rushes, forbs, mosses, lichens, and liverworts.

In May 2013, an expedition found the remains of a 10,000-year-old female woolly mammoth carcass here. They were taken to Yakutsk in the Sakha Republic for bacterial examination and tissue analysis, for a joint project with South Korea in cloning.

At Harvard in the U.S., Professor George Church has established the Woolly Mammoth Revival Team. Using the genome from frozen corpses he explores the possibility of reversing extinction by editing the genes of a close relative: the elephant.

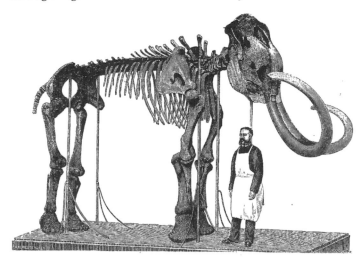

Woolly mammoth skeleton preserved in the Museum of Sciences, St Petersburg. Recovered from frozen mud in the Lena delta 1806.

# EAST SIBERIAN SEA
## *Vostochno-Sibirskoye More*

The shallow East Siberian Sea is bounded by the Laptev Sea and the New Siberian Islands to the west, Cape Billings and the Chukchi Sea to the east. There are relatively few islands but the ice brings ringed and bearded seals. Bowhead, grey, beluga, and narwhal whales summer here in pursuit of the plankton bloom of copepods and the fish they nourish. The coast was inhabited for thousands of years by indigenous tribes engaged in fishing, hunting and reindeer husbandry which eventually became absorbed first by shamanic Yakuts and later by Russians. Commercial fishing is poorly developed and there is relatively little industrial activity, resulting in relatively clean conditions.

It is the least studied of the seven Northeast Passage seas, enduring a severe foggy climate and an abundance of ice which only tends to melt in August–September. The sea freezes between October and July, becoming 2m thick in inshore waters by the end of winter. Tidal range is weak. Out in the open sea, the ice cover transforms into drifting 2–3m ice. Navigation is much hindered. Winter winds shift this treacherous ice northwards, conditions which affected the unfortunate De Long expedition.

## De Long Islands
### *Ostrova De-Longa*

Partially covered by glaciers and rising to ice-capped peaks, this is an uninhabited archipelago of five basaltic islands, lying to the east of the New Siberian Islands. U.S. citizens, independently of government, have claimed American ownership of the De Long group, based on the 1881 discovery (see 86ff). In 1916 the Russian ambassador in London issued an official notice considering Henrietta, along with other Arctic islands, integral parts of the Russian Empire. This territorial claim, unsurprisingly, was later maintained by the Soviet Union. In fact the United States government has always acknowledged the group as Russian territory.

## ZHOKOVA ISLAND *Ostrov Zhokova*
## 75°08'N 152°48'E

Zhokova was discovered in 1913 during the Imperial Russian Arctic Ocean Hydrographic Expedition led by Boris Vilkitsky in *Taimyr* and *Vaygach*. The most southerly island in the group, it is mostly level, rising smoothly by way of occasional hillocks to 123m in the centre. At the southern end there are precipitous cliffs. Anchorage is off the old polar station at the NE extremity, south of Cape Galechnyy. It was abandoned in 1993, leaving astonishing quantities of trash and scrap metal.

A low spit separates a lagoon from the sea. With luck there will be both grey and red-necked phalaropes spinning to churn plankton.

Red-necked are smaller and with a more pointed bill than the grey phalarope.

## VILKITSKY ISLAND *Ostrov Vilkitskogo*
## 75°43'N 152°24'E

*Not to be confused with the Vilkitsky Island in the Kara Sea, with the Vilkitsky island group which is part of the Nordenskiöld Archipelago in the Kara Sea, or with the Vilkitsky Island located in the Laptev Sea off the eastern shores of the Taymyr Peninsula. Vilkitsky's name is very well-represented in Arctic Russian cartography.*

Less than two km² in extent, it is the smallest in the group, with varied terrain; solid basalt, lava, and exploded scoria, ash, and pumice. It is unglaciated, likely to be open to a zodiac landing in the Arctic high summer. A five-star island full of interest.

Vilkitsky Island

The northern cliffs are 80m high, with steep stony talus slopes. Bird cliffs on the west side of the island have nesting black-legged kittiwakes, Brünnich's and black guillemots. A gently-sloping east coast has a walrus haulout of several hundred. Shingle beaches, ridge on ridge, lead to tundra with shallow ponds and a strong likelihood of Ross's gulls, fresh from the breeding colonies of the Lena delta, fossicking for aquatic larvae and gloriously indifferent to the delighted attentions of visiting birders. Wrecked boats and assorted debris, the ubiquitous rusty oil drums which betray helicopter visits, litter the area behind the beach and lead to a jumble of snow-covered boulders at the foot of the guano-streaked precipitous cliffs. On this wall of rock, auks and gulls crowd the safety of every available ledge and slope. A shortish climb and a welcome gentle slope leads to the 70m summit of the bird cliffs.

The 1968 wreck of *Inyi*, a relief ship for polar stations, lies off the spit at the SW extremity of the island.

Vilkitsky beach. Pools in the wet alder and birch scrub behind the littoral are likely places to find Ross's gull.

**Ross's gull** is the only gull with a wedge-shaped tail. Small, with a black necklace and underparts suffused a delicate pink, it is sought after by every birder, mainly because of its reclusive rarity but also on account of its beauty and graceful movement.

It is a truly Arctic bird, rarely seen south of the Arctic Circle. Rare, yet in the right place it is not only common but confidingly approachable. The location of its breeding ground was one of the great mysteries of the ornithological world until early in the 20th century. We now know that the main area is the tundra of North Yakutia, on every river delta between the Taimyr and Chukchi peninsulas. Here, Ross's gulls nest on islets in lakes and on tundra swamps some 300km north of the Arctic Circle. After breeding they move along the coast towards the Beaufort Sea coast of Alaska.

In June 1823, midshipman William Parry wrote of his shipmate James Clark Ross, *Our shooting parties have of late been tolerably successful. Mr Ross procured a specimen of gull having a black ring round its neck, and which in its present plumage, we could not find described.*

Another rarity, truly Arctic, graceful, and roughly the size of an Arctic tern, **Sabine's gull** has a black hood, black bill with yellow tip and white forked tail. Smaller than the kittiwake and more buoyant in flight, it breeds along the mainland east of the Taimyr Peninsula.

Usually, Sabine's gulls nest in a small colony, in close association with Arctic terns, taking advantage of the protection from predators provided by the aggressive terns, which harry any intruder unmercifully.

At the end of the breeding season, in August, they leave the marshy islets for a life at sea in the open Arctic ocean.

Edward Sabine was ship's naturalist in John Ross's HMS *Isabella* in 1818 when he shot and took specimens of *an elegant forktailed gull—hitherto unknown and undescribed* from a mixed colony of gulls and terns. (It was the tern-like vigorous defence of their newly-hatched chicks that made it easy to collect them.)

85

## JEANNETTE ISLAND *Ostrov Zhannetta*
## 76°47′N 158°00′E

Jeannette is the second smallest island of the group, with an area of approximately 3.3km². The domed glacier summit is at 351m. There is a narrow pebble beach at the southwest end. It was discovered in 1881, first sighted by the ill-fated Jeannette Expedition, commanded by Lieutenant Commander George W. De Long, USN.

Jeannette Island, sketch by Chief Engineer George Melville

De Long had already shown himself to be a highly competent and charismatic exploration leader. In July of 1879 he sailed from San Francisco aboard the USS *Jeannette* (formerly the Royal Navy's HMS *Pandora*), in search of North Pole glory—*the last blank space on the map*. He was pursuing the false but widely-held theory that they would emerge from the Bering Strait to penetrate a rim of Arctic ice and break through to open sea and the North Pole.

In September 1879 the expedition found they were icebound. Their vessel drifted several hundred miles with the ice, passing north of Wrangel Island. On 17 May 1881 they sighted this easternmost island of the archipelago but drifted on, towards Henrietta.

USS *Jeannette*

# HENRIETTA ISLAND *Ostrov Genriyetty*
# 77°06′N 156°33′E

Henrietta lies twenty-
five miles northwest of
Jeannette Island and
is the northernmost
of the archipelago.

Henrietta Island. From a sketch by LtCdr De Long

Roughly circular in shape, with a diameter of about 6km, much of
the island is covered with glaciers. Cape Melville is the northernmost
land for thousands of miles east and west.

The De Long expedition came here in some distress
in June 1881, when Chief Engineer George Melville took
a landing party and hoisted the national ensign, taking
possession (disputed and later withdrawn) in the name
of the United States. He constructed a cairn, enclosing
a record of their visit and reported, *the island is a desolate rock, sur-
mounted by a snow-cap, which feeds several discharging glaciers on its
east face. Dovekies nesting in the face of the rock are the only signs of
game. A little moss, some grass, and a handful of rock were brought
back as trophies. The cliffs are inaccessible, because of their steepness.*

*Jeannette* was now crushed and sunk by the unforgiving ice.
De Long and his crew had to abandon ship into three small boats
on 12 June, making for the Siberian mainland. All thirty-three of the
expedition set off in an epic tale of courage and sacrifice to reach
the Lena delta (story continues on Bennett Island).

The sinking of USS *Jeannette*

87

In 1937 a Soviet polar station was established here, closing in 1963. In 1979 the island served as the starting point for a Soviet expedition on skis to the North Pole.

## BENNETT ISLAND *Ostrov Bennetta*
## 76°40'N 149°00'E

At 60 square miles this is the largest island in the De Long group, named in 1881 for the financial backer of the Jeannette Expedition, James Gordon Bennett Jr., publisher of the *New York Herald*.

Bennett Island

The highest point of the central ice cap is 426m. Bennett has the greatest permanent ice cover within the group, with four separate glaciers perched on high, basaltic plateaux bounded by steep scarp-like slopes. All are shrinking in volume. Waterfalls cascade from the glacier snouts.

At Cape Emma (named after De Long's wife) there is an almost vertical bird cliff, seeming to be composed of giant basalt columns leaning on one another. There are stony beaches fringing the south and east coast. The tundra soils are typically moist, fine-grained, and often hummocky, bringing low-growing grasses, rushes, mosses, lichens, and liverworts. These plants either mostly or completely cover the surface of the ground. There are plenty of birds, including black and Brünnich's guillemots, black-legged kittiwakes, glaucous and Ross's gulls.

Ice sledging, bound for the safety of the Lena delta

The De Long party, sledging across the ice, camped here for eight days of comparative comfort in July 1881, *a brief respite from our distressing labors*, warmed by plentiful driftwood fires and feasting on seabird eggs and meat. All before setting out again for the New Siberian Islands of Faddeyevsky and Kotelny and a fraught small boat passage across the Laptev Strait to landfall on the Lena delta and a desolate slog over the Siberian marshland.

On a horrific journey De Long and others perished slowly—20 of the 33 crew died—with his faithfully completed journal being updated to the last. The commander of one of the other boats, Chief Engineer George Melville, survived the ordeal and eventually found what remained of De Long and his party after a protracted search. There were no survivors from De Long's boat. Melville was awarded the Congressional Gold Medal for his bravery. As Admiral in due course, he became one of the founders of the National Geographic Society. The story is told in a riveting account by Hampton Sides, *In the Kingdom of Ice*, published in 2015. Orson Welles produced a radio version of the story for CBS on 10 September 1938. (Select number 12 from archive.org/details/OrsonWelles-MercuryThe-ater-1938Recordings.)

Items from the lost vessel *Jeannette* were found off the southwest coast of Greenland three years after she had foundered, encouraging speculation that they had drifted across the pole. Fridtjof Nansen based his 1893 North Pole expedition on this thinking, believing that a specially designed ship could be frozen in the pack ice, to follow the natural drift of the polar ice along the same track as the *Jeannette* wreckage. Sailing from the New Siberian Islands, *Fram*, deliberately beset, drifted ever westward never exceeding 86°N and failing to reach the Pole, finally emerging into the North Atlantic again north of Svalbard. The icebreaker *Polarstern* has been chartered by the Wegener Institute of Bremerhaven to repeat the experiment in summer 2019 in pursuit of climate modelling information.

In 1901 the Russian Polar Expedition, led by the distinguished geologist Baron Eduard Gustav von Toll in *Zarya*, searched De Long waters for the legendary Sannikov Land, but became ice-bound. In November 1902 Toll sledged with three companions towards the mainland in search of rescue. Diaries and other artefacts were found on Bennett Island in 1903, but no sign of Toll or his party. They were never seen again. Remains of what was probably their shore base are on the east coast, in Pavla Kappena Bay.

## MEDVEZHYI ISLANDS
### Ostrova Medvezhiy

The Medvezhyi, or Bear, Islands located to the north of the mouth of the Kolyma River, are uninhabited. The coast of Siberia is some 22 miles to the southwest.

The first recorded European to report the islands' existence was the explorer Yakov Permyakov in 1710. Sailing from the Lena to the Kolyma Rivers, he recorded the silhouette of an unknown island group in the then little explored East Siberian Sea.

In 1820–1824, during Ferdinand Wrangel's Arctic expedition to the Chukchi and East Siberian Seas, he recorded traces of bear, wolf, fox, lemming and reindeer on the largest of the islands. Fyodor Matyushkin surveyed and mapped the easternmost 'Four Pillars' island, Chetyryokhstolbovoy.

Three of the four pillars

On 3 September 1878, Adolf Erik Nordenskiöld recorded that he sailed close to the island group in the steamship *Vega*. This report was made during the famous expedition that made the whole length transit of the Northeast Passage for the first time in history.

The climate is severe. There is some commercial fishing in the area though the sea surrounding the group may be obstructed by pack ice even in the summer months. In winter it is completely blocked by fast-ice.

Museum of local history and culture in Ayon village

## AYON ISLAND *Ostrov Ayon*
## 69°50′N 168°30′E

One of the largest islands in the East Siberian Sea, 63 x 38 km, separated from the mainland by the Malyy Chaunskiy Strait, Ayon is at the eastern end of the Kolyma Gulf. Generally low and flat, with many small lakes and swamps, the Chukchi people have always used its tundra as summer pasture for their reindeer herds. But as a result of decreasing government support those herds have reduced from 22,000 to around 4,000.

Ayon village is at the northwestern end, in generally poor condition, with dilapidated, unpainted buildings dating from the Soviet era. A polar station was established in 1941, encouraging settlement. Current population is about 300. There is a postal telegraph office. The lively school has a small museum of local history and culture. At the edge of the village is a demonstration yaranga. Also known as yurts, these serve as summer tents for the reindeer herders. Mostly cone-shaped, sometimes rounded, they were based on a light wooden frame, covered by sewn reindeer skins, maybe as many as fifty. Particularly large yarangas even had a smaller internal cabin.

91

## PEVEK
## 69°43'N 170°18'E

The coast east of the Kolyma River is mountainous, with steep cliffs. Settlements are few and small, with the typical population below 100. The climate is severe, summers are short and cold. The only city is Pevek (population 4,721 in 2015), the northernmost in Russia.

As the centre of a much reduced mining industry, it has exported tin and gold to Vladivostock from the port in the natural harbour of Chaunskaya Bay. Uranium, gas, and oil extraction are putative projects, along with replacing an ageing oil-fired power station by atomic power.

Pelagic cormorant

The shores and ice fields hereabouts host ringed and bearded seals and walrus as well as their predator, polar bears. Pelagic cormorants begin to be abundant on an east-going transit. Whales include bowhead, grey, beluga, and narwhal. Several *Coregonus* (whitefish) species are common, also polar smelt, cod, flounder, and Arctic char.

## CAPE SHALAUROV-IZBA *Mys Shalaurov-Izba*
## 69°51'N 174°31'E

A landing here offers a moonscape of pink granite tors. Gently rolling tundra valleys guarantee a good plant list. Ponds and elbow lakes may have sandhill cranes, grey phalarope and other waders.

Sandhill crane

Circumpolar and restricted to the far north, **Arctic foxes** wander freely over the inshore fast-ice, happy to follow a polar bear to scavenge the remains of a seal kill. Much smaller than the red fox of lower latitudes, the dog is heavier than the vixen, weighing up to 5kg/11lbs.

With its short, blunt head, small furry ears and thick insulating underfur, it will survive in temperatures as low as −70°C. Vertebrates tend to be white if they live in the far north, an adaptation to living with snow, and the Arctic fox is a perfect example, along with the polar bear and the willow grouse. But in summer they are mostly greyish-brown.

Rather solitary creatures for much of the year, they nevertheless enjoy a strong pair bond, reuniting for the breeding season at the family den which is often sited alongside a seabird colony, offering a source of prey. They may not breed at all in a year when food is scarce.

Given fast-ice or convenient ice floes to aid travel—they are perfectly capable of swimming short distances—they may cover great areas in search of seabird colonies and tideline carrion. In a hard winter they will rely to a certain extent on food they cached in the summer.

In spite of its size and conspicuous whiteness, the **snowy owl** is an elusive bird. With luck, it may be seen perched on a convenient eminence. It may even astonish by flying past a ship at sea, on passage from island to island. Adapted to extreme cold, its feet have heavily feathered pads which minimise heat loss and raise the bird off the icy ground.

They nest alone, becoming a magnet for snow geese which form a colony around the pair to benefit by protection from the foxes which they harass. Breeding success is dependent on the availability of its principal prey—lemmings. The owl hunts over marshy tundra, silently and with moth-like flight. The young owlets enjoy two lemmings a day in a good year. Adults need between 600 and 1,600 in a year to sustain them. They remain in the Arctic for the winter, unless it has been a poor lemming year in which case they migrate south, usually without much long-term breeding success.

Common over the tundra, the **Arctic lemming** is the creature often seen at the back of beaches and especially around the detritus of deserted settlements. Hamster-like, with a short tail and small eyes, the ears are tucked away in the warmth of abundant fur. Well adapted to a hard life in low temperatures and deep snow, its claws are enlarged as burrowing tools.

In favourable conditions, lemmings produce a first litter in March, while they are still under the snow. Subsequent litters of half a dozen young may appear monthly through the summer until September. They need to produce abundant offspring, since their chances of survival are not great. A good lemming year, which provides plentiful food for predators, has a profound effect on the breeding success of a number of other species, including Arctic fox, snowy owl and the skuas. For reasons which are not entirely clear, lemming populations exhibit a classic three or four-year population cycle, reaching high densities in what is known as a 'lemming year', only to crash subsequently (not by leaping off cliffs) in a steep decline resulting from food shortage, disease and stress.

The dense fur turns white in winter, at which time the lemming does not hibernate but lives along the slopes of raised beaches in a principal grass nest tunnel, with a series of side tunnels leading to foraging areas. Their main foods are grass and the leaves of Arctic willow.

They will avoid the worst of the winter cold under a blanket of snow—the nest temperature may be 22°C warmer than the outside world.

# CHUKCHI SEA
## *Chukchi More*

Named after the indigenous people, the Sea is bounded in the west by Cape Billings and Wrangel Island and to the east by Point Barrow, Alaska. Its southernmost limit is the Bering Strait which connects it to the Bering Sea and the Pacific Ocean. Vitus Bering reached it through the eponymous Strait in 1728, and in 1779 Captain James Cook came with HMS *Resolution* on his last voyage in search of a Pacific entrance to the Northwest Passage. The International Date Line crosses from northwest to southeast, displaced eastwards to avoid Wrangel Island as well as the Chukotka peninsula on the Russian mainland.

The coastal Chukchi, now joined by assimilated Yupik Eskimos (both Chukchi and Alaskan natives prefer 'Eskimo' to the Canadian

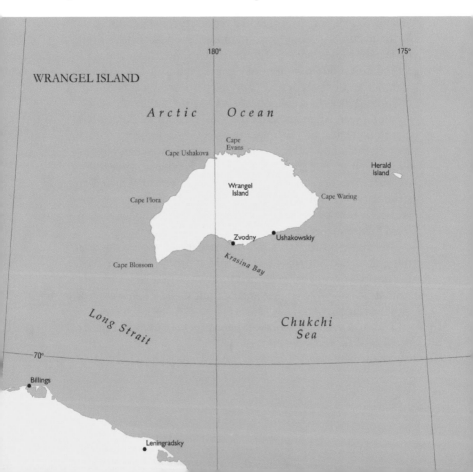

'Inuit'), traditionally engaged in fishing, walrus hunting, and whaling in this cold sea. It is navigable about four months of the year, but always there is real danger of being trapped, icebound, and carried north. There are very few islands by comparison with other Arctic seas. The principal port is Uelen.

Several oil companies competed for leases in the area, not finding enough oil and gas to be viable. There is an important military base.

## WRANGEL ISLAND *Ostrov Vrangelya* 71°20′N 179°00′W

Wrangel straddles the 180° meridian. A wide southern coastal plain is separated from a northern plain by the Tsentral'nye Mountain Range which stretches from coast to coast. It first appeared on a Russian map in 1740 but is named for Admiral Ferdinand Wrangel of the Russian Navy who saw the island, charted it but failed to land, in the 1820's. In August 1867 American whaler Thomas Long *approached it as near as fifteen miles. I have named this northern land Wrangell Land as an appropriate tribute to the memory of a man who spent three consecutive years north of latitude 68°, and demonstrated the problem of this open polar sea forty-five years ago, although others of much later date have endeavored to claim the merit of this discovery.*

Searching for the fate of the Jeannette Expedition the natural-ist John Muir came with the US revenue cutter *Corwin*. They land-ed on 12 August 1881 and claimed the island for the United States, but others disputed the claim. The icebreaker *Krasny Oktiabr* (Red October) raised the red flag in 1924, confirming Russian sovereignty.

The fishermen's settlement Ushakowsky at Rodgers Harbour *Bukhta Rodzhersa* was recognised in 1936. Summering scientists at the meteorological station and year-round wildlife rangers are part of a community of about a hundred. There is the Governor's resi-dence, a post office, store, school, a couple of monuments, and a lot of rusting oil drums. Disposal of waste is a very big problem in polar regions. In 2017 an environmental unit of the Army base collected over 1,000 metric tons of scrap metal, including 26,000 fuel barrels, for transportation and disposal to the mainland.

7,600kms$^2$ in extent, ice and fog-bound more often than is com-fortable, there are splendid cliffs, sandy beaches, shingle ridges, la-goons, a series of rivers, lowland tundra to north and south, and mountain ridges from east to west. The highest mountain is Sovets-kaya with an elevation of 1,096m. It is a world-renowned wildlife-rich sanctuary, the northernmost World Heritage Site, *Zapovednik*.

Common plants include Arctic poppy, mountain avens, Lapland butterbur, snow buttercup, villous cinquefoil, pincushion, Alpine forget-me-not, hairy lousewort, sudetan lousewort, mountain sor-rel, yellow and purple oxytrope, Alpine, stiff-stemmed, prickly and purple spider plant, tufted saxifrage, sea lungwort, glaucous wea-sel-snout, Alpine whitlow grass and northern willow among others.

Mountain avens

Biologist, husky dog, woolly rhino and muskox exhibits,
Somnitelnaya settlement, Wrangel Island

There is a staggeringly high Arctic population of 52 species of breeding birds which fluctuate in numbers but may include tens of thousands of pairs of Brünnich's guillemots and 30,000 snow goose pairs, nesting colonially, in a good season. This is one of the areas where the rare Sabine's gull might be seen. And the most westerly of the tufted and horned puffins.

Tufted puffin

Horned puffin

Rare worldwide, white-morph snow geese are well-established on Wrangel. They often settle near snowy owl or rough-legged hawk nests, discouraging predation by Arctic foxes and skuas. They winter in North America, as far south as Mexico.

As well as foxes, there are wolves. Reindeer were re-introduced in the 1950s; their numbers managed to a couple of thousand to reduce impact on ground-nesting birds. Isolated from the mainland for 6,000 years, maybe 1,000 woolly mammoths survived here until 2500-2000 BC.

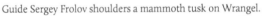

Guide Sergey Frolov shoulders a mammoth tusk on Wrangel.

Muskox

On Wrangel, muskoxen survived until possibly 2,000 years ago. In 1975, 60 were re-introduced from Nunavut in Arctic Canada. They have flourished under protection to number more than 900 today.

The island hosts the world's largest population of Pacific walrus. Haulouts on the Wrangel coast can involve more than ten thousand individuals. Marine predators, they need sea ice or beaches as resting places. Loss of summer ice over the continental shelf in recent years has increased the use of coastal beaches where they haul out in congregations which may involve tens of thousands of individuals. At this time they, and especially their calves, are highly vulnerable to disturbance. The Pacific Walrus Coastal Haulout Database has been established to monitor haulout numbers and aid conservation efforts.

Polar bears on Wrangel enjoy the highest density of breeding dens in the entire Arctic. There may be 400-500 denning in the west coast area of Cape Blossom. Summer is a time of food shortage for bears. In the recent past, 200-300 was the average population, but in 2017 a total of 589 was recorded by the island biologists. Bears are spending longer summer periods ashore on Wrangel, a consequence of the earlier ice-melt. Tideline carrion is welcome.

The inshore waters are highly productive of plankton and fish in the summer, attracting healthy numbers of bowhead, grey, and beluga whales. When the occasional whale casualty ends up on the beach it is a honeypot for bears. A zodiac party saw 230 gathered at this bowhead carcass, below, in August, 2017.

# HERALD ISLAND *Ostrov Geral'd*
## 71°23'N 175°38'W

Herald Island, SE, from USS *Corwin* 1881

Named in 1849 by Henry Kellett, captain of HMS *Herald*, this island is a rocky citadel of inaccessible cliffs and landslides, divided in two by a tundra valley with another healthy population of polar bears. The cape forming its southern extremity is some 165m high. The northwest part is higher, rising to 372m. On the beaches there are walrus haulouts. On the cliffs there is an abundance of breeding seabirds: kittiwakes, Brünnich's and black guillemots, even horned and tufted puffins.

Hazardous rocks lie close off the S, E and NW of the island. Breakers and grounded icebergs add to the unwelcoming situation. A landing leading to the interior can be made on the shore of a small bight NW of the southern extremity, the place where men from the ill-fated Karluk Canadian expedition of 1913-16 probably met their end. Government-sponsored, the scientific expedition was commanded by anthropologist Vikjalmer Stefansson in the ex-whaler

*Karluk*. On passage in the Beaufort Sea towards the planned base on Herschel Island she became trapped and drifted west, ice-bound, into the Chukchi Sea, breaking up and sinking near Wrangel Island.

Captain Robert Bartlett led what remained of the party across the ice to a cave on Herald. With an Inuit companion he reached the Siberian mainland and found his way back to Alaska to organise rescue of the survivors. A disastrous affair, the loss of eleven of the original twenty-five and the subject of much controversy.

The **gyrfalcon** is the most northerly of breeding falcons, well established along the Northeast Passage. The female is somewhat larger than the male—tiercel—but both are big, the largest of the falcons. Colour and size vary from dark grey-brown to white. In fact they are trimorphic, with three distinct colour phases. The white phase occurs most commonly in the north of the range. They hold vast territories, breeding on the ledges of cliff crags, tucked under an overhang in a mountainous habitat, usually not far from the larder of a bird colony.

They hunt fast and low in sparrowhawk fashion, taking birds by surprise, sometimes by aerial stoop. The principal prey is ptarmigan and willow grouse, but they may also take lemmings and hares. Opportunists, they will prey on auks, gulls and terns. There is always the chance of finding one perched high in the rigging of a ship, keeping a watch for likely prey. Once safely on the ground, or high in the rigging, they break the neck or tear the head off their prey.

In autumn they will take advantage of flocks of small birds, such as snow buntings. Most winter north of 65°N, even spending time on sea ice, far from land.

Many thousands of eyasses (fledglings) have been taken from the nest in the past by collectors but also for museum specimens. The white morph, which is usually larger than the grey, is greatly prized in falconry. Medieval Norwegian kings presented them as prestige gifts to diplomats, monarchs and popes.

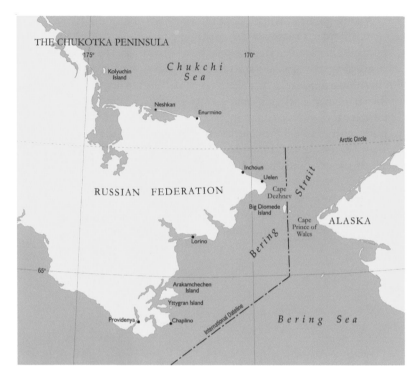

## KOLYUCHIN ISLAND *Ostrov Kolyuchin*
## 67°28′N 174°37′W

Kolyuchin is a small and uninhabited island, 4.5 x 1.5km, off the Chukotka Peninsula. In 1878, the Swedish explorer Adolf Erik Nordenskiøld overwintered and mapped here during the first transit of the Northeast Passage in the SS Vega. The pebble beach and a stiff climb lead to a 1930's Soviet polar station which was abandoned in 1993. Subsequently, the dilapidated site has been pillaged.

There is typical tundra vegetation, tufted slopes with a profusion of high summer floral colour. Black fleabane, Lapland butterbur, nodding lynchnis, boreal Jacobs ladder, grass of Parnassus, Arctic daisy, cloudberry and Arctic cinquefoil can be found.

The island's sea cliffs and spectacular stacks offer nest ledges for vast numbers of Brünnich's guillemots, kittiwakes, glaucous gulls and pelagic cormorants. Pacific puffins, both horned and tufted, are found here in fair numbers at the extreme west of their range.

A settlement, Kolyuchino, at the southern end of the island, survived till 1987. Originally the small number of eskimo inhabitants scraped a living from the seasonal bird bonanza and by hunting walrus (walrus remains are scattered over the tundra vegetation). Archaeological research revealed that the Chukchi villagers, following the shamanistic religion, made a ritual circle of walrus skulls. Late 18th century immigration by settlers from the south introduced trade with Alaska. From Nome came trade goods, the return cargo was of skins, furs and mammoth tusks. As the American bowhead whale fishery flourished at the turn of the century, crew-hungry whaler captains called at islands like Kolyuchin in search of prime seamen, reared on the walrus hunt. Kolyuchin hunters found themselves bound even further west, as far as Franz Josef Land, in pursuit of even larger marine mammals.

Kolyuchin Island's abandoned meteorological station

On Kolyuchin Island, near-vertical cliffs and stacks offer narrow ledges for a seabird city of Brünnich's guillemots. The single egg is laid on bare rock. It is pear-shaped, pyriform. This has been assumed to be an adaptation which allows them to spin like tops to avoid falling over the edge if disturbed.

In a somewhat explosive experiment carried out by a Russian scientist, Stanislav Uspensky, in 1948, a series of gunshots were fired deliberately to panic a breeding colony early in the season. This resulted, not surprisingly, in a cascade of eggs falling from the ledges. But later in the season, though the birds took fright and flew off, *not a single egg tumbled off the ledge*. He claimed that freshly laid eggs roll off the ledge without a problem if disturbed, but as they are incubated and the embryo develops, the air space expands at the larger end, shifting the centre of gravity to the pointed end, causing the egg to spin round the pointed end rather than fall off. So the egg is most likely to come to grief at the early stage of incubation, in which event the female simply lays another and starts again, with another chance for success.

Today's ornithologists are unconvinced and say that they are still not sure why the egg is pyriform.

## NESHKAN
## 67°02'N 172°58'W

Neshkan is situated on a sandy spit between a lagoon and the sea. It took its name from the Chukchi word meaning 'Seal's head' (after the aspect of a local mountain viewed from the sea). The village, population 700, was founded as the result of Soviet efforts in the 50's to encourage itinerant reindeer herders into a collective. Exploitation of oil and gas brought some benefit (a number of multi-story houses were built in the village in 2005, a direct result of the oligarch Roman Abramovich's tenure as Governor of Chukotka). However, the region, at the northern boundary of the Bering plate, is subject to seismic disturbance. A seismic swarm near the village lasted over two years in 2003/4, with events of magnitudes up to 3.0. Surface deformities are common.

The village economy still depends on reindeer herding, supplemented by fishing, but it suffers from remoteness and its lack of transport infrastructure, being 250 km from Lavrentiya, the district centre.

Not far from Neshkan, uninhabited Idlidlya Island 67°02'N 172°46'W is an important wildlife monitoring site. It has a thriving walrus colony, strict protection legislation bars vessels from approaching closer than twelve miles.

# ENURMINO
## 66°57′N 171°52′W

On the Chukotka mainland the Enurmino village dates from about 500 AD, home for a population of about 300 today. A fine sandy beach leads to the single hard-packed dirt street serving an enclave of wooden buildings. There are the remains of a fox farm. Today the villagers are reindeer herders and hunters harvesting walrus and bowhead whales when they get the chance. An annual quota allows for a catch of three whales, thirty walrus and unlimited seals. There is a food store, an elementary school, a daycare centre and a post-office. A supply helicopter calls every couple of weeks.

The best wildflowers are at the cemetery. Boreal Jacob's ladder, monkshood, bluebell, marsh fleabane, scurvygrass, cottongrass, mountain heliotrope, Actic raspberry, Arctic daisy, nodding saxifrage. In this area of Chukotka, there are 356 species of flowering plants (3 in the equivalent Antarctic latitude, 100,000 in the tropics!).

Amundsen overwintered here in the bay with *Maud* 1920–1921 in the course of his aborted 1918–1921 Northeast Passage eastbound expedition. Finally reaching Nome in Alaska, she was bought by the Hudson's Bay Company. Renamed *Baymaud*, she ended up rotting quietly in the mud of Cambridge Bay, Nunavut, until a grand plan raised the hulk in the summer of 2016 to wait for a tow back home to the Fram museum in Oslo.

Amundsen's *Maud*, wintering in Enurmino

Raised from her muddy slumber, *Maud* under tow in August 2017 for refit in Oslo.

Anadyr-born director Aleksei Vakhrushev made a 60 minute documentary 'Welcome to Enurmino!' which was premiered in Canada in 2008. It deals with the lives of the inhabitants, showing the villagers trying to preserve their traditional ways of life while making the most of the limited modern amenities available to them.

## INCHOUN
## 66°18′N 170°17′W

Inchoun lies alongside a lagoon enclosed by two sand spits which allow access for small boats through a narrow channel. Archaeological excavations at a creekside site by the local Heritage Centre and the State Museum of Northern Art have shown that this area has been inhabited for at least 3,000 years. The present-day population of fox farmers and marine hunters is around 400. The fox farm is in some disarray as a consequence of the world-wide anti-fur lobby.

Chukchi coastal marine communities have always maintained close relations with the reindeer herders of the inland tundra. Nowadays the inhabitants have moved out of their reindeer-hide *yarangas* and into more permanent houses, though also wood-framed! A well-stocked general store offers visitors the opportunity to buy locally-made fur and walrus souvenirs. In the streets, drying-frames process fish. At one time Inchoun is said to have had the best Soviet reading room hereabouts. There is a thriving primary school for those at the early stages of learning before they move on to the larger establishment at Uelen.

Yaranga tents in 1885

# UELEN
## 66°10′N 169°48′W

The Cape Dezhnev peninsula was a centre for trade between American and Russian whalers and walrus hunters and the native Yupik and Chukchi coastal trappers of the late 19ᵗʰ and early 20ᵗʰ centuries. So for many years its town of Uelen—the most easterly settlement in the whole of Eurasia and the closest Russian settlement to the United States—was an important trading port for both American and Russian fur and ivory entrepreneurs.

The town is on the northeast corner of a lagoon, separated from the ocean by a substantial sandspit. Population according to the most recent census was 740. This regional seat of government is a lively place, serving as a base for both polar science and archaeological expeditions to the area covering a time span from 500 BC to AD 1000. Excavations have shown that Uelen was a major settlement in the area in the first few centuries AD, as well as revealing the existence of a culture that has always been dependent on whale and walrus hunting.

Since early times Uelen has been a major artistic centre famed on both sides of the Bering Strait for furs and walrus ivory carving. Today there is a thriving cultural scene including the world's only museum of walrus ivory carving. Unconnected by road to any other part of the world it is nevertheless a bustling and successful town.

Uelen

Umiaks at Uelen. Traditional 6–10m long open boats, double-ended, driftwood or whalebone-framed and covered with walrus or bearded seal skins. Their shallow draft makes them convenient for beaching and overturning as shelters. They can carry several tonnes of freight or move people and possessions to seasonal hunting grounds; along with kayaks they are used in hunting walrus and whales.

## CAPE DEZHNEV *Mys Dezhnevya*
## 66°05′N 169°39′W

The northernmost point of Eurasia, Cape Dezhnev marks the transition from the Chukchi Sea to the Bering Strait. Passing as he tried to reach the Beaufort Sea in 1778, Captain James Cook called it the Eastern Cape. In 1898 it was renamed in honour of Semyon Dezhnev, the Cossack sailor who had rounded it in 1648, long before Bering reached these waters.

The 804m cape appears as an island from a distance, but is the tip of a rocky headland connected to the mainland and the village of Uelen by a neck of low-lying land of swamps and shallow lakes.

On landing, a steep grassy wildflower slope leads to a high plateau and circles outlined in stone and colonised by squirrels. Little is left of Naukan, the Yupik village abandoned in 1958 on account of its poor anchorage. There is a bronze monument to Semyon Dezhnev, serving as a lighthouse. Other Russian sailors are honoured by commemorative crosses.

At Cape Dezhnev the Yupik village of Naukan was inhabited for 2000 years until abandoned in 1958. The 400 or so inhabitants were relocated to various Chukchi settlements. Their language, intermediate between that of central Siberia and Alaska, is still spoken by a few of the remaining Naukans. Their earliest dwellings used whale jawbones as framework supports for a skin roof.

# BERING STRAIT
## *Proliv Bering*

Between Cape Dezhnev and the Alaskan Cape Prince of Wales, the Bering Strait spans about 50 miles. It is assumed that in the Pleistocene, when lower ocean levels exposed the sea floor, Yupik Paleo-Indians migrated across a land bridge we now know as Beringia. In more recent centuries geographers presumed a 'Strait of Anian'. Semyon Dezhnyov confirmed it in 1648, Vitus Bering in 1728. It is the gateway to the Bering Sea.

The US-Russia boundary is marked by longitude 168° 58' 37" W, where for convenience the International Date Line runs between the Diomede Islands. This leaves the Russian and American sides with different calendar days. During the Cold War this border became known as the 'Ice Curtain'. Today, the Russian coast of the Bering Strait is a closed military zone, open to foreigners only with special permits and clearance from Providenya or Anadyr.

Through the years adventurers have tried to walk on ice, swim, ski, sledge or drive amphibious vehicles across and there have been grandiose plans to dam, bridge or tunnel. Unauthorized arrivals risk prompt deportation or fines, even a taste of prison. One of the more common dangers faced by conventional mariners is the prevalence of hazardous logs drifting in the strong currents.

Big and Little Diomede

## BIG DIOMEDE *Ostrov Ratmanova*
## 65°47'N 169°04'W

The easternmost point of Russia, Big Diomede is the larger of the two small islands in the middle of the Bering Strait. Semyon Dezhnyov claimed to land here in 1648, it was re-discovered by Vitus Bering in 1728 on 16 August, the day on which the Russian Orthodox Church celebrates the memory of the martyr St Diomede. There is an important weather station, a military presence and a population of some 2,000 in an Eskimo village.

In 1867 the Russian/American border was drawn between the islands, making tiny Little Diomede, with its population of 100 Chukchi in the village of Ignaluk, just a couple of miles further east, part of Alaska.

Both islands are bordered by imposing cliffs. It is not easy, and sometimes not permitted, to land. On the other hand, there may be the chance of sailing close to a beach crowded with literally a thousand walrus.

Big Diomede

**Grey whales** are scarred by parasites which perish in the Arctic feeding grounds of the Bering and Chukchi Seas, where an eastern North Pacific population summers in relatively healthy numbers, while a separate Asian population is critically endangered. A single individual was recorded in the Mediterranean in 2010, 200 years after Atlantic extinction, perhaps having found its way through the Northwest Passage! There is talk of a plan to airlift surplus Pacific animals to repopulate the Atlantic.

The mottled grey-white body distinguishes them from other whales. The tapered head leads to a robust body. Like the bowhead, they lack a dorsal fin, just a hump and a string of knuckles, an adaptation convenient for working under ice.

They are shallow-water feeders, turning on their right sides to scoop sediment, sucking it to filter small crustaceans and tubeworms through the baleen sieve. Dives last three to five minutes, sometimes longer. There may be a trail of mud in

the wake of a foraging whale. The 4m blow is heart-shaped. It breaches and spyhops, showing diagnostic fluke spots on diving.

They make one of the longest annual migrations of any mammal, travelling some 5,000 miles along the western seaboard of North America to calve and winter in warm Baja Californian waters. In the past they were heavily exploited by the whaling industry (called devilfish by whalers on account of their ferocity). Since 1947 they have enjoyed protection, at least on paper. Aboriginal subsistence whaling in the Bering and Chukchi Seas resumed in 1948 and has continued into the present, apart from an interruption in the early 1990s during the collapse of the USSR.

# LORINO
## 65°29'N 171°41'W

With a population of well over a thousand this is the largest village on the coast, even larger than the administrative centre Lavrentiya,

The *Lorino Dawns* native ensemble

40 kilometers away by unpaved road. Originally known as the Yupik settlement of Nukak, it was first recorded in the 18th century. As with most Chukotkan villages, the main occupations are fishing, whaling and reindeer herding. Fox farming has been important in the past. A processing factory for seafood and meat canning was opened in 2009. There is a high school, a daycare centre, a boarding school, a cultural centre, a co-op, a hospital and post office. The Lorinski hot springs are 15 km from the village.

Landing beach at Lorino

## ARAKAMCHECHEN ISLAND *Ostrov Arakamchechen* 64°55′N 172°31′W

Just north of Cape Chaplino and eight kms off the coast of Chukot-ka, the main settlement on this island is Yanrakynot, a traditional Chukchi village built alongside a spit on the west side of the en-trance to the Venetken Lagoon. Whaling dominates the economy, harvesting passing migrants, some greys, but mostly the more easily harpooned bowheads. Walrus have mainly been hunted for their meat but also importantly for the ivory of their tusks. The animals were easily taken as the ice retreated north in summer when an old male might be resting on the beach carrying more than 5kg of ivory (tusks of the Pacific walrus are much larger than those of the Atlan-tic subspecies). In times past, even diplomatic bags carried walrus ivory as coveted gifts to foreign potentates.

The population of several hundred Chukchi includes some Yupik Eskimo. The important meat store benefits from the permafrost. There is a school, a dispensary, a post office. There is even an unpaved road leading fifty miles to Providenya. It is a lively and welcoming place where they are well-used to tourist visitors. These might be entertained by dancing, but also by sports such as sledge-jumping, reindeer antler lassoing, or wrestling.

There will be a chance to buy soapstone carvings, walrus tusks, fox pelts, or reindeer boots. However, the walrus is protected by law nowadays. It is illegal to export walrus parts (or narwhal tusks) without the legal certificate.

In the case of the recov-ering Pacific subspecies some subsistence hunt-ing is permitted. Perhaps 5,000 are estimated to be taken annually, on both sides of the border, either legally or poached. But with elephant ivory politically unacceptable and only illegally marketed, the unfortunate walrus may again become the target of ivory-hunters, placing their slow recovery in jeopardy.

**Bowhead whales** move north—as far as 75°N—to give birth in the spring, when the ice breaks up. Slow swimmers, at about three knots, they feed on surface plankton at the edge of the pack. They have a very large mouth, equipped with the longest baleen plates among the world's whales—up to 3m long—to sieve vast quantities of krill, copepods, and pteropods. They have no dorsal fin, an adaptation to working under ice. In surfacing to breathe, they tend to show two distinct curves in profile as they reveal themselves for the double blow half a dozen times in two or three minutes, before sounding for 20 minutes. The tail flukes are thrown high as they slide under. On occasion they may lift the massive head clear of the water, showing a white bib.

Although a truly Arctic species, the bowhead is decidedly uncommon. An endangered species, yet it has been shown that an individual may live 200 years. Their great size, and the fact that they float when killed, made them desirable prey for early

whalers (in the days before compressed air kept carcasses afloat). Bowheads were hunted for blubber and oil, but specially prized for the value of their extra long 'whalebone', the baleen bristles. Cut into narrow strips and inserted into lining, they became 'stays', the understructure for bodices and corsets in the fashion industry. Originally abundant, the whales were exploited to near-extinction from the 17th century. In spite of protection for over 90 years the population is still barely holding its own. The greatest number is confined to the Chukchi Sea, one of the few sea areas where bowheads are almost common and there may be some 7,000. But, as the autumn ice advances, they retreat to winter as far south as 55°N.

Bowheads have a massive bony skull which serves to break through as much as 60cm of solid ice. Arranged in a ritual circle, as at Ittygran, skulls can be seen on several of the islands of the Chukchi peninsula.

## YTTYGRAN ISLAND *Ostrov Yttygran*
## 64°37'N 172°35'W

Separated from the mainland by a mile, this is home for a fascinating archaeological site. Fur seals, grey and bowhead whales are common here, hunting the inshore waters. Lying on their migration route, the whales have been subject to a long-established harvest. Anchorage tends to be off the west side, but the famous Whale Bone Alley is below low cliffs and high bluffs on a wide coastal plain in the northeast. A stone path leads to the carefully arranged ritualised lines of bowhead whale skulls. Jawbones, vertebrae and ribs are associated with meat storage pits. It is an ancient festival site, celebrating harvest time. The local Yupik believe that the island was a major centre for the flensing, butchery, and storage of whale meat, the Yupik name *Sikliuk* meaning 'meat pit' (flesh was dried, rolled and fermented in the pit for winter use, acquiring the much-appreciated sour taste).

Lemmings and ground squirrels approve of the plentiful tunnels associated with the whalebones. Arctic plants are abundant. There are hot thermal pools on the tundra.

Nearby islets are a magnet for zodiac cruises and abundant seabirds, especially Pacific puffins.

Chukchi ceremonial burial sites date from the 14th century Little Ice Age, but petroglyphs date from earlier millenia. In Chukchi shamanism, spirits populate the universe, speaking to the shaman in casting spells and predicting the future. Since most activity took place in the home, shamanism suffered less than the other religions from the Soviet government's antireligious policies.

*The Chukchi people believe the Earth was created from raven droppings; the first woman bore whale-children and from them came the Chukchi people.*
—Yuri Rytkheu

## NUNEANGAN ISLAND *Ostrov Nuneangan*
## 64°37′N 172°20′W

Nuneangan Island is just three miles from Yttygran and with a jolly orange navigation cabin on its grassy summit, this little islet offers a bird bonanza. Bluff on all sides and with only tiny beaches, zodiac circumnavigation reveals many thousands of nesting seabirds: pelagic cormorants, glaucous gulls, kittiwakes, guillemots and a fair sprinkling of horned and tufted puffins. At dusk, the sky is almost darkened in a spectacular aerial display by auklets.

Crested auklets

## NEW CHAPLINO *Novoye Chaplino*
## 64°30'N 172°51'W

On the north shore of Tkachen Bay, the New Chaplino village offers a sheltered anchorage. It is an ancient settlement and whaling centre close to Providenya. Population was 419 in 2010, mostly Chukchi or Yupik. The Chaplino hot-springs are a local attraction.

Abandoned whaling station at New Chaplino

## PROVIDENYA
## 64°25′N 173°15′W

Providenya is a deep-water port that benefits from a sheltered fjord, close to the southern limits of the winter ice fields but normally ice-free between mid-June and the end of November. It was primarily established to provide bunkering and general facilities for vessels navigating the Northern Sea Route.

One of the original houses in Providenya

Many of the current population of nearly 2,000 are Yupik. There is a museum of regional history and culture, a technical school, cinema, post office, bakery complex, and one of the only two ski slopes in Chukotka.

From Providenya Bay airport there are services to both Nome and Anchorage in Alaska.

To the south lies the Pacific Ocean and the fabled East: the final objective of the Northeast Passage. Five hundred years of exploration and now a significant ice retreat make it possible for the traffic which was always dreamt of: a rich opportunity for well-found, ice-hardened vessels to reveal a largely unexplored region of wildlife islands.

*Strange. There is always sadness on departure. It is as if one cannot after all bear to leave this bleak waste of ice, glaciers, cold and toil...* —Fridtjof Nansen 1912

# Appendices

## PLANTS

The first surprise when landing on an Arctic beach is the paucity of littoral plants. Where you expect to see various wracks and low-water kelps, there is nothing but a beach scraped clean by moving ice. Once behind the beach, though, there is life, sometimes in profusion.

The landscape of the High Arctic is determined by permafrost. Where it is continuous the ground is frozen for several hundred metres down. Only in summer is the top metre melted enough to create a poorly drained marshy soil with a certain amount of dry country. Arctic plants must therefore adapt to the harsh conditions of winter when there is intense frost, yet endure summer temperatures which may reach as high as 30°C.

Arctic plants face a short growing season, intense cold, wind, low nutrients in the soil, and the 'feast or famine' nature of the water. Yet the short Arctic summer is a carnival of colour in miniature, as the ground-hugging plants flower briefly. Frozen under snow for most of the year, they find a way to exist under even the most extreme conditions.

Moss campion

## Noteworthy plants of the Northeast Passage
List compiled by Judy Lasca

Arnica, Alpine *Arnica alpina*
Avens, Entire-leafed *Dryas integrifolia*
    Mountain *D. octopetala*

Butterbur, Lapland *Petasites frigidus*
Buttercup, Arctic *Ranunculus hyperboreus*
    Northern *R. affinis*
    Snow *R. nivalis*
Campion, Moss *Silene acaulis*
Capitate Valerian *Valeriana capitata*
Chickweed *Stellaria crassipes*
Cinquefoil, Snow *Potentilla nivea*
    Arctic *P. hyparctica*
    Villous *P. villosa*
Cloudberry *Rubus chamaemorus*

Cotton Grass, Arctic *Eriophorum scheuchzeri*
Cotton grass, Common *E. angustifolium*
Cuckoo-flower *Cardamine pratensis*
Daisy, Arctic *Chrysanthemum arcticum*
Dandelion, Smooth *Taraxacum glabrum*
Draba, Snow *Draba navies*
Fireweed, Arctic *Epilobium angustifolium*

Broad-leafed *E. latifolium*
Fleabane, Black *Erigeron humilis*
Forget-me-not, Arctic *Eritrichium aretioides*
Gentian, Arctic *Gentiana propinqua*
    Glaucous *G. glauca*
Harebell, Arctic *Campanula uniflora*
Heather, White Arctic Bell *Cassiope tetragona*
Hedysarum, Alpine *Hedysarum alpinum*
Heliotrope, Mountain Valeriana sitchensis
Horsetail, Common *Equisetum arvense*
Jacob's Ladder, Boreal *Polemonium boreale*

Knotweed *Polygonum viviparum*
Larkspur, Northern Dwarf *Delphinium brachycentrum*
Lousewort, Capitate *Pedicularis capitata*
    Hairy *P. hirsata*
    Sea, *P. maritima*
    Sudetan *P. sudetica*
Mastodon flower *Senecio congestus*
Meadow-grass, Alpine *Poa alpina*
Monkshood *Aconitum delphinifolium*
Nodding Lynchis *S. wahlbergella*
Mouse-ear, Arctic *Cerastium arcticum*
Narrow-leafed Saussurea *Saussurea angustifolia*

Northern Water Carpet *Chrysosplenium alternifolium*
Oxytrope, Yellow *Oxytropus monticola*

Parnassus, Grass of *Parnassia palustris*
Parsnip, Cow *Heracleum lanatum*
Pea, Beach *Lathyrus maritimus*
Pincushion *Diapensia lapponica*

Pink Plumes *Polygonum bistorta*
Poppy, Arctic *Papaver radicatum*
Primrose, Chukchi *Primula tschuktschorum*
Roseroot *Sedum rosea*

Sandwort, Alpine *Minuartia rubella*
Saxifrage, Alpine *Saxifraga nivalis*
    Brook *S. punctata*
    Bog *S. hirculus*

Bulblet *S. cernua*
Nodding *S. cernua*
Prickly *S. tricuspidata*
Purple *S. oppositifolia*
Spider Plant *S. flagellaris*
Stiff-stemmed *S. hieracifolia*
Tufted *S. caespitosa*

Seabeach Sandwort *Arenaria peploides*
Scurvy-grass, Common *Cochlearia officinalis*
Sorrel, Mountain *Oxyria digyna*
Stitchwort, Long-stalked *Stellaria longipes*
Thrift *Armeria maritima*
Whitlow-grass, Lapland *Draba lactea*
Willow, Arctic *Salix arctophila*
    Least *S. herbacea*
    Net-veined *S. reticulata*
    Polar *S. polaris*
Wormwood, Tilesius's *Artemesia tilesii*

## Lichens

Mane lichen *Alectoria nigricans*
Pixie cup *Cladonia asahinaea*
Map lichen *Rhizocarpon geographicum*
Worm lichen *Thamnolia sp.*
Rock tripe *Umbilicaria sp.*

Jewel lichen *Xanthorina elegan*

## BIRDS

Few birds are resident year-round in the High Arctic, winter conditions are too severe. The plumage of the very few resident Arctic species is denser than that of seasonal visitors. Ivory gulls keep company with foxes and polar bears in order to benefit from scraps. Snowy owls will not breed at all in a year when lemmings are scarce. Snow buntings and willow grouse dig snow holes in order to crouch out of the wind. In extreme cold birds will tuck both their legs and heads under the feathers.

Willow grouse

But this inhospitable region is seasonally home to some of the largest wader and seabird populations in the world. As the sunlight returns in spring, there is a huge influx of birds from the south. One hundred and eighty-three species breed in these high latitudes, taking advantage of the short but immensely productive summer season of abundance.

In the breeding season courtship tends to be brief, with nests constructed and eggs laid at the earliest possible moment. Swans, geese, and ducks, along with a host of waders—shorebirds—graze the meadows and hunt the midge and mosquito larvae in tundra pools. Eiders and terns must wait until the ice breaks up to expose the ground and isolate their offshore islands from predatory foxes. Seabirds nest in 'bazaars' along the high cliffs and forage for copepods and small fish far out to sea. They tend to nest sociably; their eggs and meat taste good. Easy access to southern bird colonies has led to centuries of persecution in which the attitudes of mainlanders and islanders have differed sharply. Peoples in remote regions have a keen awareness of the importance of the seasonal boost to their economy and husband it carefully. Survival of human populations in the far north, depended, and still to a certain extent, depends, on the summer influx of birds. They are an important food source, but also traditionally provided materials for clothing and bedding.

Seabird populations are notoriously subject to violent fluctuations. A late break-up of the ice may deny food to breeding birds and cause mass starvation. A late thaw may even mean that whole populations of seabirds fail to breed successfully. Pirates like glaucous gulls and skuas harry other birds. All take maximum advantage of the twenty-four hours of daylight, since the summer season of plenty is short.

They don't overstay their welcome. Summer breeders tend to be off to the milder south by the end of August, though fulmar fledglings may still be on their ledges in early September. If the few days of autumn arrive early, juveniles may be unready to flee from the onset of winter. The autumn moult may even be delayed in order to make an early getaway and leave winter behind.

Brünnich's guillemots

## Noteworthy birds of the Northeast Passage

(NB: Americans use common names which sometimes differ from those in Europe. This list, in taxonomic order, has the American version in brackets.)

| Scientific | English | Russian |
| --- | --- | --- |
| Gavia stellata | Red-throated diver (loon) | Krasnozobaya gagara |
| Fulmarus glacialis | Northern Fulmar | Glupysh |
| Cygnus columbianus | Bewick's swan (tundra) | Maly lebed |
| Anser caerulescens | Snow goose | Bely gus |
| Branta bernicla | Brent goose (brant) | Chjernaya kazarka |
| B.leucopsis | Barnacle goose | Beloschokaya kazark |
| Somateria mollissima | Eider | Obyknovennaya gaga |
| S.spectabilis | King eider | Gaga-grebyonushka |
| Clangula hyemalis | Long-tailed duck | Moryanka |
| Buteo lagopus | Rough-legged buzzard | Zimnyak |
| Falco peregrinus | Peregrine | Sapsan |
| F. rusticolus | Gyrfalcon | Krechet |
| Lagopus lagopus | Willow grouse | Belaya kuropatka |
| Grus canadensis | Sandhill crane | Kanadsky zhuravl |
| Pluvialis squatarola | Grey plover | Tuless |
| Charadrius hiaticula | Ringed plover | Galstuchnik |
| Arenaria interpres | Turnstone (ruddy) | Kamnesharka |
| Calidris maritima | Purple sandpiper | Morskoy pesochnik |
| C. ferruginea | Curlew sandpiper | Krasnozobik |
| C. alpina | Dunlin | Chernozobik |
| C. minuta | Little stint | Kulik-vorobey |
| C. melanotos | Pectoral sandpiper | Dutysh |
| C. alba | Sanderling | Peschanka |
| C. canutus | Knot | Pesochnik |
| Phalaropus fulicarius | Grey phalarope | Ploskonosy plavunchik |
| P. lobatus | Red-necked phalarope | Kruglonosy plavunchi |
| Stercorarius pomarinus | Pomarine skua (jaeger) | Sredny pomornik |
| S. parasiticus | Arctic skua (jaeger) | Korotkokhvosty pomornik |

| | | |
|---|---|---|
| *S. longicaudus* | Long-tailed skua (jaeger) | Dlinnokhvosty pomornik |
| *Larus hyperboreus* | Glaucous gull | Burgomistr |
| *Rhodostethia rosea* | Ross's gull | Rozovaya chayka |
| *Xema sabini* | Sabine's gull | Vilokhvostaya chayka |
| *Rissa tridactyla* | Black-legged kittiwake | Moevka |
| *Pagophila eburnean* | Ivory gull | Belaya chayka |
| *Sterna paradisaea* | Arctic tern | Polarnaya krachka |
| *Alle alle* | Little auk (dovekie) | Lyurik |
| *Uria lomvia* | Brünnich's guillemot (thick-billed murre) | Tolstoklyuvaya kayra |
| *Cepphus grille* | Black guillemot | Chistik |
| *Aethia cristatella* | Crested auklet | Bolshaya konyuga |
| *Fratercula arctica* | Atlantic Puffin | Tupik |
| *F. corniculata* | Horned puffin | Ipatka |
| *F. cirrhata* | Tufted puffin | Toporik |
| *Nyctea scandiaca* | Snowy owl | Belaya sova |
| *Calcarius lapponicus* | Lapland bunting (longspur) | Laplansky podorozhnik |
| *Plectrophenax nivalis* | Snow bunting | Poonochka |

Snow buntings

## MAMMALS

Few land-based mammals can endure the Arctic winter with its 24 hours of darkness, freezing cold, and scarce food. Those which survive are specially adapted to extreme climatic conditions, blessed with extra-thick pelage and well covered extremities. Insulated against the cold, their main winter problem is finding enough to eat. None of them hibernate; they are active throughout the year. One welcome advantage is that any left-over prey from the days of summer plenty will remain in good condition in the refrigerated days of winter. In times of hardship even herbivores may become carrion-eaters.

Those mammals which depend on the ocean environment live in profoundly different conditions. While lemmings, muskoxen and foxes must find ways of dealing with temperatures down to -50°C, seals and whales bask in water which can never dip below -2°C. They face one serious problem, however. Dependant on a supply of fresh air for breathing, they must have access to the open air. Polynyas may provide an answer, and they are a mecca for many animals, but in ice-bound waters they must break through the ice to create breathing holes or drown.

Narwhals

Predecessors of the modern Eskimo made use of caches, hunted reindeer, and fished for char. They also hunted seals over the ice in winter. Superbly adapted to the rigours of life in a hostile environment, their tools were made from bones, their clothing—key to survival—from bird skins and mammal hides, sinew and gut. As land-based hunters they used sleds hauled by reindeer or huskies—domesticated wolves. Huskies still serve as hunting companions in the days of snowmobiles, adept at sniffing out seal pups hidden by snow. They also serve as guards, warning of polar bears.

In summer, hunters worked at sea, fishing and spearing seals and whales. The traditional diet was low in carbohydrate, high in protein and even higher in fat. It was almost sugar-free: heart problems are still rare among them. They enjoyed plant material and berries when they were available. Necessary vitamins were no problem even in winter; their vitamin C came from raw seal liver and *muktuk* (whale skin and blubber).

## Noteworthy mammals of the Northeast Passage

| | |
|---|---|
| Arctic ground squirrel | *Spermophilus parryi* |
| Common lemming | *Lemmus sibiricusi* |
| Wrangel lemming | *L. s. portenkoi* |
| Arctic fox | *Vulpes lagopus* |
| Polar bear | *Ursus maritimus* |
| Ringed seal | *Pusa hispida* |
| Harp seal | *Pagophilus groenlandicus* |
| Bearded seal | *Erignathus barbatus* |
| Walrus | *Odobenus rosmarus* |
| Muskox | *Ovibus moschatus* |
| Reindeer | *Rangifer tarandus* |
| Bowhead whale | *Balaena mysticetus* |
| Grey whale | *Eschrichtius robustus* |
| Narwhal | *Monodon monoceros* |
| Beluga | *Delphinapterus leucas* |

In the Great Bear constellation, Dubhe and Merak point the way
to the pole star Polaris. Engraving by Sidney Hall in 1824.

*The Terrestrial North Pole is the northernmost point on Earth, lying
diametrically opposite the South Pole, where Earth's axes intersect with
the surface. It defines geodetic latitude 90° North. All lines of longitude
converge there, all directions point south. Along tight latitude circles,
counterclockwise is east and clockwise is west. The pole is surrounded by
the Arctic Ocean where the maximum depth is 4,261m and it is mostly
covered with drifting ice 1.8 to 3m (6-10') thick. Current predictions
suggest that the North Pole may become seasonally ice-free on account
of Arctic ice shrinkage, with timescales varying towards the late 21st
century. (The magnetic North Pole is defined as the point in the Northern
Hemisphere where the Earth's axis of rotation meets the surface.*

136

# Svalbard and Franz Josef Land

played an important part as staging posts in

# The Race for the Pole

In 1606 the cartographer Gerardus Mercator, benefitting from Barents's charts, produced a map (see p8) which proposed an Open Polar Sea. The assumption was that because the sun shone throughout three months in the high northern summer, the ice would melt and a ship could make it across the 'top of the world'.

The Muscovy Company of England took up the challenge *Inasmuch as it hath pleased Almighty God, to discover unto our nation a land, lying in 80° toward the North Pole: we are desirous, not only to discover farther to the northward along the said land, to finde whether the same doth trend, either to the eastward or to the westward of the Pole; as also whether the same be inhabited by any people, or whether there be an open sea farther northward than hath already been discovered. A passage maybe as soon attayned this way by the pole as any unknowne way whatsoever.*

In 1607, they commissioned the navigator Henry Hudson to sail on the first of May for the pole with a crew of ten men and a boy on the 80-ton *Hopewell*. Coasting West Spitsbergen on 13 July, he estimated that they had reached 80° 23'N, more probably 79° 23'. Thinking the land would stay with them, when in reality it trended to the east, they held to the northern course, encountered unpassable ice and were forced to turn back. The expedition returned to Tilbury on the Thames on 15 September, having inevitably failed to reach the Pole.

One of the Company's sealer skippers was Jonas Poole. After showing his prowess on several trips to Bear Island they commissioned him to return for yet more walrus skins but in addition they required him to penetrate higher and *proceed northward from thence, to search for the likelihood of a trade or passage that way.*

He sailed in 1610 with the 70 ton *Amity*, with a crew of fourteen. After three months working the west coast of Spitzbergen, which, like Barents, he identified as Greenland, he shaped a course for the north. Finding fog and ice he fell in with the impenetrable ice-field, skirted towards the west, never finding an opening, but reaching 79° 50', probably exceeding Hudson's highest latitude. Finding impassable ice and 'seeing no prospect of a passage', he turned back, prudently collecting a cargo of walrus hides and the baleen of stranded bowheads, confirming Barents's news of 'great store of whales'. Escaping subsequent shipwreck with difficulty and many broken bones, on return to London he was 'miserably and basely murdered'. In truth his trip had been more successful in hunting than opening a way to the pole.

## Enter the Navy

In June 1773 the British Admiralty sent Constantine Phipps, the 2$^{nd}$ Baron Mulgrave, off from Deptford in the bomb-ketch HMS *Racehorse* on a voyage towards the North Pole and possible passage to the Pacific. His second in command was Skeffington Lutwidge, with HMS *Carcass*. Benefiting from an influential uncle, fifteen year old Horatio Nelson found himself one of her midshipmen. The expedition reached 80° 37'N, a record at that time, but, unable to find a way through close pack ice, was forced to turn back in September. Lutwidge later said that while the ship had been trapped in the ice, Nelson had seen and pursued a polar bear, before being ordered to return on board. On being questioned about his recklessness, he replied 'I wished, Sir, to get the skin for my father'.

Middy Nelson's musket misfired. A shot from *Carcass* frightens the bear off.

At the end of the eighteenth century little or nothing was known of the topography of the extremes of the polar world. In the early years of the nineteenth, geographic exploration was rudely interrupted by the Napoleonic Wars. When Bonaparte was exiled to St Helena in 1815 Britain's Royal Navy was left with a triumphant and flourishing fleet without an immediate challenge to its supremacy and with a lot of redundant ships and sailors keen to distinguish themselves. Exploration came to the rescue. Polar regions became a proving-ground for masculinity and patriotism. However, the British was not the only navy with an interest.

In 1820 Ferdinand Friedrich Georg Ludwig Freiherr von Wrangel was appointed by the Imperial Russian Navy to command the *Kolymskaya Expedition* to explore the Siberian polar seas. Leaving Nizhnekolymsk in the Sakha Republic on 1 November 1823 he dog-sledged forty six days over the ice, reaching 72°2' N. He returned to St. Petersburg on 15 August 1824 from an expedition which made valuable research in glaciology, geomagnetics and climatology but failed to find an open polar sea.

## Parry and his farthest north

In 1825 Lieutenant William Edward Parry persuaded the Admiralty to back an attempt on the North Pole. With HMS *Hecla*, this was the first voyage to set out with the explicit intention of reaching the North Pole. In 1827 they cleared the northern extremity of Spitsbergen to reach impenetrable ice at latitude 82°45'N, setting a record for exploration that stood for nearly five decades. Testing the possibility of sledge operations, they found that almost as fast as they hauled their sledges northward, the ice flowed southward in a somewhat discouraging manner. Following this

William Edward Parry, 1821

HMS *Hecla*

failed attempt at the pole, *Hecla* was withdrawn from Arctic service, but Parry was knighted and continued to serve the navy with distinction, finally as head of the department of steam machinery. Arctic exploration lost its attraction till in pursuit, not of the pole but yet again the Northwest Passage, came the British navy's ill-fated Franklin expedition of 1845. Sailing from London in May, *Erebus* and *Terror* reached into the archipelago from the Davis Strait in August only to be lost to the world. It was nearly ten years before their fate was discovered, by John Rae of the Hudson Bay Company. Both ships had come to grief with the loss of all hands, one hundred and twenty-nine souls. Between 1847 and 1859 at least 36 expeditions were involved in the search by both land and sea. Some were epic failures. More ships and men were lost looking for Franklin than in the Franklin Expedition itself. Arctic exploration lost its attraction yet again for the British Admiralty for another fifteen years.

## Enter the Americans

A grant of $50,000 from the U.S. Congress sponsored an American attempt to be the first to reach the North Pole. The explorer Charles Francis Hall had already tried twice to solve the Franklin mystery when he was chosen to command the USS *Polaris* for an expedition which ended in disaster. Sailing in September 1871 they wintered in northwest Greenland. By this time the party had split into rival factions, with Hall's authority resented by many of the party, and discipline broke down. Beaten by the inevitable ice, *Polaris* turned back to the Greenland coast. In October the ship was beset. On the verge of being crushed, the crew abandoned ship. Drifting for six months on an ice floe they travelled over 1,500 miles to be rescued off the coast of Newfoundland by the sealer *Tigress* and find safety ashore in April 1873 at St. Johns. It is likely that all would have perished had the group not included several Inuit who were able to hunt for the party.

## The warm polar sea

Until well into the nineteenth century, it was commonly believed that only a barrier fringe of heavy ice barred the way to a tepid sea and new lands. Ferdinand von Wrangel had looked for land in the far north of Siberia. He couldn't find any but noted a Chuckchi chief saying 'One might on a clear summer's day descry snow-covered mountains at a great distance to the North'. The chief exponent of the theory of this convenient gateway of warm water to the pole was the German geographer August Heinrich Petermann, who influenced a generation of mid-century explorers. His preference was for ship-based exploration rather than the British and American enthusiasm for sledging.

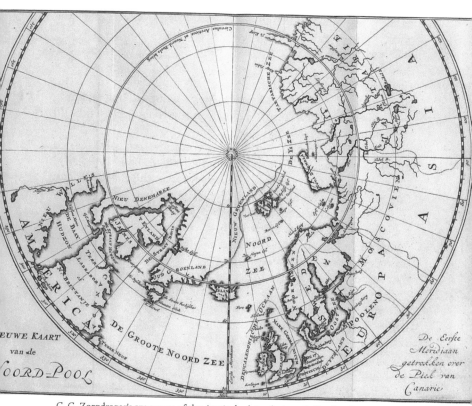

C. G. Zorgdrager's 1720 map of the Arctic, hedging bets and allowing for possible land extending north of Greenland.

## The western approach

In 1875, still inclined to believe in an open polar sea, the Admiralty sent HM ships *Alert* and *Discovery* for the British Arctic Expedition, led by Sir George Strong Nares. Sailing from Portsmouth, they attempted to reach the North Pole via the Davis Strait and Smith Sound. They emerged beyond Greenland and Ellesmere Island to find a wasteland of impenetrable ice. They contented themselves with exploring those northern coasts and collecting scientific data. With a dog-sledging party, Commander Albert Hastings Markham reached 83°20'26"N, passing Parry's Farthest North record but

HMS *Alert*

the expedition was a near-disaster. Poorly equipped and suffering from scurvy, the men seemed unlikely to survive another winter in the ice and so retreated.

Three American and one British expedition gradually pushed out from the shores of Greenland and Ellesmere Land to 83°24'N. Unfortunately, these extra degrees were won at the cost of at least three ships and over fifty men—a high price indeed.

Driftwood wreckage from the USS *Jeannette* of the De Long expedition (see p 86) was found three years after she sank on the coasts of Svalbard and Greenland, showing that ocean currents flowed the Arctic from east to west and encouraging speculation that associated ice sheets drifted across the pole itself. In Norway, Fridtjof Nansen based his 1893 North Pole expedition on this assumption. Proposing a ship which he would deliberately beset, to drift west with the current towards the pole and eventually reaching open sea between Greenland and Spitsbergen, he persuaded both the Norwegian Geographical Society, government and public, to back his plan.

Naval engineer Colin Archer was employed to design and build a sturdy vessel of the toughest oak. Its rounded hull was designed to squeeze the ship upwards rather than to be crushed when gripped by ice. Sailing efficiency was seen as less important than the provision of a safe and warm shelter for the predicted confinement and inevitable monotony.

Launched in October 1892, *Fram* sailed the Northeast Passage to the New Siberian Islands. When they approached the area in which *Jeannette* foundered, Nansen headed north into the ice before stopping engines at 78°49'N 132°53'E, lifting the rudder out of harm's way. Deliberately beset, frozen in, the drift began in September 1893.

*Fram* leaving Bergen, bound for the Arctic, 2 July 1893

Drifting at the mercy of the currents, the icebound vessel rarely made more than a mile a day and never exceeded 86°N. Admitting that they would not reach the Pole courtesy of the current, in March 1895 Nansen and Hjalmar Johansen left the ship and sledged to reach it on skis. A month later, after reaching 86°13'6"N (almost three degrees beyond the existing record), realising they were going to run out of food and seeing a *veritable chaos of iceblocks stretching as far as the horizon* they abandoned the attempt. They turned back south to sledge for safety, reaching what Nansen tentatively identified as the western edge of Franz

March 1894, beset and drifting

Josef Land (in fact what we now know as Jackson Island) towards the end of August. As the weather grew colder they had no choice but to camp for the winter. In a sheltered cove, with driftwood, stones and moss for building materials, the pair made a shallow excavation and built a stone-walled hut, roofed with a ridgepole draped with walrus skins. This was to be their home for the next eight months. With enough ammunition, availability of bear, walrus and seal to keep the larder stocked, their problem was not so much hunger as inactivity. Kayaking to Cape Flora in June 1896, Nansen heard a dog barking. He went to investigate, to meet explorer Frederick Jackson. In one of life's classic encounters, on meeting *a tall man, wearing a soft felt hat, loosely made voluminous clothes, with long shaggy hair and beard*, Jackson asked 'You are Nansen, aren't you?'.

'Yes, I am Nansen'

Jackson was camped at Cape Flora on nearby Northbrook Island, where his expedition had a sub-base. On 7 August, Nansen and Johansen boarded their supply ship *Windward*, sailing for Vardø on the east coast of Norway. Here they were greeted by Hans Mohn, one of the proponents of the polar drift theory, who was in the town by chance. The world soon knew of Nansen's safe return, though as yet there was no news of *Fram*. But in that same month, on 18 August, came the news that she had emerged from the ice northwest of Spitsbergen, as Nansen had predicted. She had not passed over the pole, nor exceeded Nansen's northernmost position. Nansen and Johansen sailed for Tromsø, where they were reunited with their comrades.

Meanwhile, back at their main base on Northbrook island the Jackson-Harmsworth Expedition completed the highly successful survey which was their main work, showing that the archipelago extended no higher north than 81°, with Rudolf the northernmost Island. (Jackson had been misled by earlier maps into believing that Franz Joseph Land was a land mass that probably extended to the North Pole).

## First aerial attempt

In 1897 the Swede Salomon Andrée, joined by Nils Strindberg and Knut Frænkel, tried to cross over the Pole and the top of the world in the hydrogen balloon *Örnen* (Eagle). By all accounts the expedition was ill-advised, involving an untested, leaky, balloon, ineffective drag-rope steering and an over-optimistic leader who ignored advice.

Taking off from Danes Island

Taking off in July 1897 from Danes Island in Northwest Svalbard the balloon came to grief on the unforgiving pack ice two days later. Unhurt, but inadequately prepared, they faced a gruelling trek back towards land. As the Arctic winter closed on them in October, they came to the uninhabited Kvitøya (White Island) in the Northeast of Svalbard. They died there, alone, three months later, their fate an unsolved riddle till on 6 August 1930 sealers with the Norwegian Bratvaag Expedition landed to find the remains of a campsite, skeletons, graves disturbed by bears and the expedition's logbooks. A media sensation erupted in Sweden, where the intrepid explorers had been seen as heroes.

Time has modified their reputations. Andrée's optimism, faith in the power of technology, and disregard for the forces of nature are seen to have led to led to his death and those of his two companions.

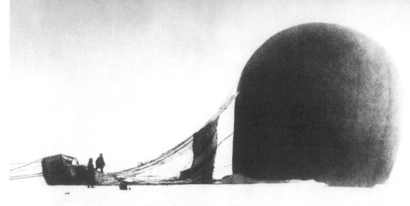

Two days later

## More sledging

On 12 July 1899 Luigi Amedeo, Duke of the Abruzzi, and Admiral Umberto Cagni of the Royal Italian Navy, sailed north from Archangel with the vital sled dogs aboard the steam whaler *Stella Polare*, for Franz Josef Land. Basing their expedition at Rudolf Island in the extreme north, trouble came in winter when their ship was badly damaged and Amedeo was injured by frostbite. The expedition's physician had to amputate two of the royal duke's fingers and the maimed commander was pronounced unfit to lead the polar attempt. Command fell to Cagni, who set off on 11 March,

12 July 1899, *Stella Polare's* crew on departure from Archangel

with dogs hauling food and supplies for a three-month march. Reaching latitude 86°34' on 25 April, the sledge party planted a flag to set a new record exceeding by 35 km Nansen's 1895 farthest north of 86°14'. But the four men of the Cagni party came to realise that, short of food, the North Pole was beyond their reach. Turning back, and twelve days after their projected survival deadline, they regained their base on 23 June.

On 16 August the damaged *Stella Polare* left Rudolf Island for Norway, returning to Italy in triumph, with Cagni lionised.

## Byrd's overflight attempt

US naval officer Richard E. Byrd's earlier experience of flying over sea ice and glaciers in western Greenland fired his ambition to fly over the North Pole. The first claimed flight was made on 9 May 1926. Byrd, acting as navigator with pilot Floyd Bennett in a Fokker tri-motor aircraft, flew from King's Bay, Spitsbergen, to the Pole and back. The flight lasted 15½ hours, with no mishaps beyond an oil leak from the starboard engine of their aircraft. For this feat they were both awarded the U.S. Congressional Medal of Honor and were acclaimed as national heroes.

Fokker VII

Verified at the time by a committee of the National Geographic Society, this claim has since been undermined by scrupulous refereeing and the 1996 revelation that long-hidden diary data consistently contradict Byrd's report.

## Undisputed overflight

The first consistent, verified and uncontroversial attainment of the Pole was the brainchild of polar explorer and expedition leader Roald Amundsen on 12 May 1926. Finance for the trip came from the American explorer Lincoln Ellsworth along with the Aero Club of Norway, to be known as the Amundsen-Ellsworth 1926 Transpolar Flight. They used the Norwegian semi-rigid dirigible airship *Norge*, re-inforced for Arctic conditions and powered by three engines, designed and piloted by the Italian Air Force officer Umberto Nobile. With helmsman Oscar Wisting, navigator Hjalmar Riiser-Larsen, and the expedition's sponsor, Lincoln Ellsworth, their flight started from Ny Ålesund in Svalbard and crossed the Arctic Ocean by way of 90°N to Alaska. Nobile overflew the Pole a second time on 24 May 1928, in the airship *Italia*, which crashed on its return from the Pole, with the loss of half the crew, possibly a result of sleep deprivation.

Amundsen's dirigible *Norge* at Ny Ålesund

## Drifting past the pole

In May 1937 the drifting ice station, *North Pole 1*, first of an annual series, was established by Soviet Union scientists thirteen nautical miles from the Pole. Led by Ivan Papanin, for the next nine months oceanographers, meteorologists and radio operators carried out scientific research at the station which must have passed over or very close to the Pole. On 19 February 1938, when the group was picked up by the icebreakers *Taimyr* and *Murman*, their station had drifted 2850 km to the eastern coast of Greenland. More recently, the Russians have established an annual drifting base, *Barneo*, close to the Pole. This operates for a few weeks during early spring. Today you can fly in by plane or helicopter to a well-maintained landing strip near the pole.

Russian-operated and with an integrated ice runway, it caters for scientific researchers as well as tourists who take advantage of flights from Longyearbyen in Svalbard and a helicopter to the pole.

Ice station Barneo

## First to set foot

The first men definitely to set foot at the North Pole were from a Soviet party organized by the Chief Directorate of the Northern Sea Route (which lies inside Russia's domestic waters - a major part of the Northeast Passage), which included geophysicists and oceanographers and the flight crew of Aleksandr Kuznetsov's Sever 2 expedition. The party flew from Kotelny Island in the Russian far East and landed three Lisunov Li-2s on 23 April 1948. They established a temporary camp and for the next two days conducted scientific observations. On 26 April the team flew back to Siberia. A year later, on 9 May 1949, two other Soviet scientists, Vitali Volovich and Andrei Medvedev, became the first people to parachute onto the North Pole, jumping from a Douglas C-47 Skytrain.

## First submarine visit

The United States Navy's USS *Nautilus* SSN 571 was the first submarine to sail under the polar ice, passing below the North Pole on 3 August 1958. She is now preserved in the Submarine Museum in Groton, Connecticut. On 17 March 1959 the USS *Skate* SSN 578 became the first to break through the ice, in the manner of a bowhead whale, to surface at the North Pole.

On 17 March 1959 USS *Skate* surfaced at the North Pole

## First by snowmobile

Ralph Plaisted and three companions, Walt Pederson, Gerry Pitzl and Jean-Luc Bombardier, travelled over the ice by snowmobile, parking at 90°N on 19 April 1968, their position confirmed independently by the United States Air Force.

## First to walk there

Sledging from Point Barrow, Alaska, on 21 Feb 68, Wally Herbert and companions Allan Gill, Roy Koerner and Kenneth Hedges of the *British Trans-Arctic Expedition* became the first men to reach the Pole on foot, with the help of four sledges, forty dogs and airdrops on 6 April 1969 (the 60th anniversary of Robert Peary's disputed expedition!). They continued on to complete the first surface crossing of the Arctic Ocean by its longest axis, ending in Svalbard 29 May 1969; a feat that has not been repeated. Wally Herbert was knighted in 2000, one of the last explorers of the polar regions who was able to make major contributions to geographical discovery and research.

First to reach the pole on foot, the British Trans-Arctic Expedition of 1969

Seascape at 90°N

The concept of an 'open polar sea' allowing ship navigation over the pole was almost an assumption from the early 17th century till nearly the end of the 19th. It was commonly believed that only a barrier fringe of heavy ice barred the way to a tepid sea and new lands. Many ships tried and failed to reach the goal. The 20th century proved the magnitude of problems involved in the desire to stand at the pole, culminating in Wally Herbert's sledging achievement in 1969. Only the arrival of the immensely powerful nuclear icebreakers made it possible for surface vessels to reach the pole.

## First surface vessel

On 17 August 1977 the Soviet nuclear-powered icebreaker *Arktika* became the first surface ship to reach the North Pole.

*Arktika*

Subsequent nuclear icebreakers of the Russian fleet carried polar tourists annually to disembark onto the ice at 90°N in midsummer.

## Useful websites

AECO (Assoc. of Arctic Expedition Cruise Operators): aeco.no
Arctic Research Institute, St Petersburg: aari.ru
British Admiralty charts: admiralty.co.uk
Expedition cruise consultancy: expeditionvoyage.com
EYOS, superyacht expeditions: eyos-expeditions.com
National Oceanic & Atmospheric Administration: arctic.noaa.gov
Northern Sea Route Offices, Murmansk and Kirkenes: arctic-lio.com
Sea ice graphs: sites.google.com/site/arcticseaicegraphs/
Sea ice news and analysis: nsidc.org/arcticseaicenews/
Yacht consultancy: highlatitudes.com info@highlatitudes.com

## Charts

The co-ordinates quoted in this book are inevitably rough and
    ready, a situation not unknown in the Arctic Ocean, but they
    relate to islands and not fixed points.
British Admiralty 4006 is a useful passage chart.
U.S. charts 804 and 800 cover Greenland to the Kara Sea and Kara
    Sea to Bering Strait. nauticalcharts.noaa.gov.
Russian charts, geospacial.com, gunio@homepage.ru, offer the
    best coverage. 10100 to 10105 cover the NSR in large-scale.
Small scale charts are listed on pages 7 and 8 of the 8th edition of
    the Admiralty Sailing Directions NP10.

## Selected references

Alexander, Philip *The North-West and North-East Passages* CUP 1915

Alford, S. *London's Triumph: Merchant Adventurers* Allen Lane 2017

Arctic Pilot Vol 1 UK Hydrographic Office 2010

Barrow, John *A Chronological History of Voyages Into the Arctic Regions* John Murray 1818

Belapol'skii, L.O. *Ecology of Seabirds in the Barents Sea* 1961

Bering Sea Pilot UK Hydrographic Office 2013

Bland, Richard *Early Art of the Far East* Anchorage 2007

Capelotti, P.J. *By Airship to the North Pole* Rutgers UP 1999

—— *Shipwreck at Cape Flora* UP Calgary 2013

Cunnane, Jarlath *Northabout* Collins 2005

De Long, Emma *The Loss of the Jeannette* Houghton Mifflin 1884

De Veer, Gerrit *The Three Voyages of William Barents* Hakluyt 1876

Flint, V.E. *Birds of the USSR* Princeton UP 1984

Herbert, Wally *Across the Top of the World* Longmans 1969

Johnson, H. *The Life and Voyages of Joseph Wiggins* John Murray 1907

Keupp, Marcus *The Northern Sea Route* Springer 2015

Mayers, Kit *Northeast Passage to Muscovy* Sutton 2005

McKinlay, W.L. *The last voyage of the Karluk* St Martin's Press 1999

Mills, Wm J *Exploring Polar Frontiers* ABC-CLIO 2003

Muir, John *The Cruise of the Corwin* Houghton Mifflin 1917

Nansen, Fridtjof *Farthest North* Harper 1897

Nobile, U. *With the Italia to the North Pole* Allen & Unwin 1930

Nordenskiöld, A.E. *The Voyage of the Vega* Macmillan 1881

Østreng, Willy *Shipping in Arctic Waters* Springer 2013

Parry W *Narrative of the Attempt to reach the North Pole*

Peel, Helen *Polar Gleams* Arnold 1894

Ross, Sir John *In Search of the Northwest Passage* London 2010

Seebohm, Henry *The Birds of Siberia* John Murray 1880

Sides, Hampton *In the Kingdom of Ice* Oneworld 2015

Starokadomskiy, L.M. *Charting the Russian Northern Sea Route* McGill-Queens UP 1976

Toomey, Capt. Patrick *The Ice Navigation Manual* Witherby 2010

Transport Ministry, Russian Federation *Navigating the Northern Sea Route* 1996

Welzl, Jan *Thirty Years In the Golden North* Macmillan 1932

Zdor, Eduard *Traditional knowledge of walrus* Anadyr 2010

# Picture Credits

Page numbers in *italics* refer to pictures in the public domain. Those marked **bold** are by the generous courtesy of colleagues and shipmates.

# Acknowledgements

Mike Messick, Darrel Schoeling, Susan Adie and Laurie Dexter opened my eyes years ago to the delights and disasters of expedition leading. But I also owe a huge debt to those who have helped to improve my understanding of this fascinating part of the world. Historians Bob Headland and Ian Stone, geologists Norm Lasca and John Splettstoesser, botanists Stephen MacLean and Judy Lasca, ice pilot Captain Pat Toomey; Andrey Gostnikov, Nikolai Drozdov and Fabrice Genevois have all been shipmates. I remember with gratitude those guests on Arctic expeditions whose unexpected expertise has illuminated glorious sea days as well as the occasional grim ones. Mike Salisbury knew when to reach for the reviving bottle. I need to acknowledge the awesome skills of icebreaker Captains Oleg Agafonov of *Kapitan Dranitsyn*, Alexander Lembrick of *Yamal*, and Yevgeniy Bannikov of *Sovetskiy Soyuz* in tackling heavy pack ice and pressure ridges in search of ice-capped islands, tundra lagoons, walrus haulouts and seabird cities. And a special warmth for Hilary Bradt, who encouraged me to write about those rewarding places.

**Polite comments, corrections, and additions will be gratefully acknowledged: tonysoper@icloud.com**

# Index

Main entries are in **bold**, illustrations in *italic*

# INDEX

# Other guides by Tony Soper

## Antarctica, a guide to the wildlife
### Bradt 2018 (7th edn)

*Few people can claim to be thoroughly familiar with Antarctic wildlife. Most of us visiting the deep south are doing so for the first time and thirst for some authoritative guidance. Here...is the book we have been waiting for.*
—Sir David Attenborough

*For anyone Antarctica-bound, this is the book.*
—Keith Shackleton

## The Arctic, a guide to coastal wildlife
### Bradt 2019 (4th edn)

*The best wildlife coverage of any of the guide books.*
—BBC Wildlife

*Beautifully written, engaging text.*
—WWF Wildlife bulletin

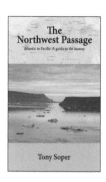

## The Northwest Passage
### Venture Books 2019

*An excellent practical guide, giving both a historical perspective as well as an account of the situation today.*
—Jens Karl Holm

.

Printed in the USA
CPSIA information can be obtained
at www.ICGtesting.com
LVHW080752011023

759528LV00019B/2